Epictetus

The Stoics

THE BIG NEST

THE BIG NEST

LONDON · NEW YORK · TORONTO · SAO PAULO · MOSCOW
PARIS · MADRID · BERLIN · ROME · MEXICO CITY · MUMBAI · SEOUL · DOHA
TOKYO · SYDNEY · CAPE TOWN · AUCKLAND · BEIJING

New Edition

Published by The Big Nest
This Edition first published in 2016
Copyright © 2018 The Big Nest
All Rights Reserved.
ISBN: 9781787247130

CONTENTS

THE ENCHIRIDION   7
THE DISCOURSES   26
THE GOLDEN SAYINGS   144
THE HYMN OF CLEANTHES   230

THE ENCHIRIDION

1. Some things are in our control and others not. Things in our control are opinion, pursuit, desire, aversion, and, in a word, whatever are our own actions. Things not in our control are body, property, reputation, command, and, in one word, whatever are not our own actions.

The things in our control are by nature free, unrestrained, unhindered; but those not in our control are weak, slavish, restrained, belonging to others. Remember, then, that if you suppose that things which are slavish by nature are also free, and that what belongs to others is your own, then you will be hindered. You will lament, you will be disturbed, and you will find fault both with gods and men. But if you suppose that only to be your own which is your own, and what belongs to others such as it really is, then no one will ever compel you or restrain you. Further, you will find fault with no one or accuse no one. You will do nothing against your will. No one will hurt you, you will have no enemies, and you not be harmed.

Aiming therefore at such great things, remember that you must not allow yourself to be carried, even with a slight tendency, towards the attainment of lesser things. Instead, you must entirely quit some things and for the present postpone the rest. But if you would both have these great things, along with power and riches, then you will not gain even the latter, because you aim at the former too: but you will absolutely fail of the former, by which alone happiness and freedom are achieved.

Work, therefore to be able to say to every harsh appearance, "You are but an appearance, and not absolutely the thing you appear to be." And then examine it by those rules which you have, and first, and chiefly, by this: whether it concerns the things which are in our own control, or those which are not; and, if it concerns anything not in our control, be prepared to say that it is nothing to you.

2. Remember that following desire promises the attainment of that of which you are desirous; and aversion promises the avoiding that to which you are averse. However, he who fails to obtain the object of his desire is disappointed, and he who incurs the object of his aversion wretched. If, then, you confine your aversion to those objects only which are contrary to the natural use of your faculties, which you have in your own control, you will never incur anything to which you are averse. But if you are averse to sickness, or death, or poverty, you will be wretched. Remove aversion, then, from all things that are not in our control, and transfer it to things contrary to the nature of what is in our control. But, for the present, totally suppress desire: for, if you desire any of the things which are not in your own control, you must necessarily be disappointed; and of those which are, and which it would be laudable to desire, nothing is yet in your possession. Use only the appropriate actions of pursuit and avoidance; and even these lightly, and with gentleness and reservation.

3. With regard to whatever objects give you delight, are useful, or are deeply loved, remember to tell yourself of what general nature they are, beginning from the most insignificant things. If, for example, you are fond of a specific ceramic cup, remind yourself that it is only ceramic cups in general of which you are fond. Then, if it breaks, you will not be disturbed. If you kiss your child, or your wife, say that you only kiss things which are human, and thus you will not be disturbed if either of them dies.

4. When you are going about any action, remind yourself what nature the action is. If you are going to bathe, picture to yourself the things which usually happen in the bath: some people splash the water, some push, some use abusive language, and others steal. Thus you will more safely go about this action if you say to yourself, "I will now go bathe, and keep my own mind in a state conformable to nature." And in the same manner with regard to

every other action. For thus, if any hindrance arises in bathing, you will have it ready to say, "It was not only to bathe that I desired, but to keep my mind in a state conformable to nature; and I will not keep it if I am bothered at things that happen.

5. Men are disturbed, not by things, but by the principles and notions which they form concerning things. Death, for instance, is not terrible, else it would have appeared so to Socrates. But the terror consists in our notion of death that it is terrible. When therefore we are hindered, or disturbed, or grieved, let us never attribute it to others, but to ourselves; that is, to our own principles. An uninstructed person will lay the fault of his own bad condition upon others. Someone just starting instruction will lay the fault on himself. Some who is perfectly instructed will place blame neither on others nor on himself.

6. Don't be prideful with any excellence that is not your own. If a horse should be prideful and say, " I am handsome," it would be supportable. But when you are prideful, and say, " I have a handsome horse," know that you are proud of what is, in fact, only the good of the horse. What, then, is your own? Only your reaction to the appearances of things. Thus, when you behave conformably to nature in reaction to how things appear, you will be proud with reason; for you will take pride in some good of your own.

7. Consider when, on a voyage, your ship is anchored; if you go on shore to get water you may along the way amuse yourself with picking up a shellish, or an onion. However, your thoughts and continual attention ought to be bent towards the ship, waiting for the captain to call on board; you must then immediately leave all these things, otherwise you will be thrown into the ship, bound neck and feet like a sheep. So it is with life. If, instead of an onion or a shellfish, you are given a wife or child, that is fine. But if the captain calls, you must run to the ship, leaving them, and regarding none of them. But if you are old, never go far from the ship: lest, when you are called, you should be unable to come in time.

8. Don't demand that things happen as you wish, but wish

that they happen as they do happen, and you will go on well.

9. Sickness is a hindrance to the body, but not to your ability to choose, unless that is your choice. Lameness is a hindrance to the leg, but not to your ability to choose. Say this to yourself with regard to everything that happens, then you will see such obstacles as hindrances to something else, but not to yourself.

10. With every accident, ask yourself what abilities you have for making a proper use of it. If you see an attractive person, you will find that self-restraint is the ability you have against your desire. If you are in pain, you will find fortitude. If you hear unpleasant language, you will find patience. And thus habituated, the appearances of things will not hurry you away along with them.

11. Never say of anything, "I have lost it"; but, "I have returned it." Is your child dead? It is returned. Is your wife dead? She is returned. Is your estate taken away? Well, and is not that likewise returned? "But he who took it away is a bad man." What difference is it to you who the giver assigns to take it back? While he gives it to you to possess, take care of it; but don't view it as your own, just as travelers view a hotel.

12. If you want to improve, reject such reasonings as these: "If I neglect my affairs, I'll have no income; if I don't correct my servant, he will be bad." For it is better to die with hunger, exempt from grief and fear, than to live in affluence with perturbation; and it is better your servant should be bad, than you unhappy.

Begin therefore from little things. Is a little oil spilt? A little wine stolen? Say to yourself, "This is the price paid for apathy, for tranquillity, and nothing is to be had for nothing." When you call your servant, it is possible that he may not come; or, if he does, he may not do what you want. But he is by no means of such importance that it should be in his power to give you any disturbance.

13. If you want to improve, be content to be thought foolish

and stupid with regard to external things. Don't wish to be thought to know anything; and even if you appear to be somebody important to others, distrust yourself. For, it is difficult to both keep your faculty of choice in a state conformable to nature, and at the same time acquire external things. But while you are careful about the one, you must of necessity neglect the other.

14. If you wish your children, and your wife, and your friends to live for ever, you are stupid; for you wish to be in control of things which you cannot, you wish for things that belong to others to be your own. So likewise, if you wish your servant to be without fault, you are a fool; for you wish vice not to be vice," but something else. But, if you wish to have your desires undisappointed, this is in your own control. Exercise, therefore, what is in your control. He is the master of every other person who is able to confer or remove whatever that person wishes either to have or to avoid. Whoever, then, would be free, let him wish nothing, let him decline nothing, which depends on others else he must necessarily be a slave.

15. Remember that you must behave in life as at a dinner party. Is anything brought around to you? Put out your hand and take your share with moderation. Does it pass by you? Don't stop it. Is it not yet come? Don't stretch your desire towards it, but wait till it reaches you. Do this with regard to children, to a wife, to public posts, to riches, and you will eventually be a worthy partner of the feasts of the gods. And if you don't even take the things which are set before you, but are able even to reject them, then you will not only be a partner at the feasts of the gods, but also of their empire. For, by doing this, Diogenes, Heraclitus and others like them, deservedly became, and were called, divine.

16. When you see anyone weeping in grief because his son has gone abroad, or is dead, or because he has suffered in his affairs, be careful that the appearance may not misdirect you. Instead, distinguish within your own mind, and be prepared to say, "It's not the accident that distresses this person., because it doesn't distress another person; it is the judgment which he makes about it." As far as words go, however, don't reduce

yourself to his level, and certainly do not moan with him. Do not moan inwardly either.

17. Remember that you are an actor in a drama, of such a kind as the author pleases to make it. If short, of a short one; if long, of a long one. If it is his pleasure you should act a poor man, a cripple, a governor, or a private person, see that you act it naturally. For this is your business, to act well the character assigned you; to choose it is another's.

18. When a raven happens to croak unluckily, don't allow the appearance hurry you away with it, but immediately make the distinction to yourself, and say, "None of these things are foretold to me; but either to my paltry body, or property, or reputation, or children, or wife. But to me all omens are lucky, if I will. For whichever of these things happens, it is in my control to derive advantage from it."

19. You may be unconquerable, if you enter into no combat in which it is not in your own control to conquer. When, therefore, you see anyone eminent in honors, or power, or in high esteem on any other account, take heed not to be hurried away with the appearance, and to pronounce him happy; for, if the essence of good consists in things in our own control, there will be no room for envy or emulation. But, for your part, don't wish to be a general, or a senator, or a consul, but to be free; and the only way to this is a contempt of things not in our own control.

20. Remember, that not he who gives ill language or a blow insults, but the principle which represents these things as insulting. When, therefore, anyone provokes you, be assured that it is your own opinion which provokes you. Try, therefore, in the first place, not to be hurried away with the appearance. For if you once gain time and respite, you will more easily command yourself.

21. Let death and exile, and all other things which appear terrible be daily before your eyes, but chiefly death, and you win never entertain any abject thought, nor too eagerly covet anything.

22. If you have an earnest desire of attaining to philosophy, prepare yourself from the very first to be laughed at, to be sneered by the multitude, to hear them say,." He is returned to us a philosopher all at once," and " Whence this supercilious look?" Now, for your part, don't have a supercilious look indeed; but keep steadily to those things which appear best to you as one appointed by God to this station. For remember that, if you adhere to the same point, those very persons who at first ridiculed will afterwards admire you. But if you are conquered by them, you will incur a double ridicule.

23. If you ever happen to turn your attention to externals, so as to wish to please anyone, be assured that you have ruined your scheme of life. Be contented, then, in everything with being a philosopher; and, if you wish to be thought so likewise by anyone, appear so to yourself, and it will suffice you.

24. Don't allow such considerations as these distress you. "I will live in dishonor, and be nobody anywhere." For, if dishonor is an evil, you can no more be involved in any evil by the means of another, than be engaged in anything base. Is it any business of yours, then, to get power, or to be admitted to an entertainment? By no means. How, then, after all, is this a dishonor? And how is it true that you will be nobody anywhere, when you ought to be somebody in those things only which are in your own control, in which you may be of the greatest consequence? "But my friends will be unassisted." -- What do you mean by unassisted? They will not have money from you, nor will you make them Roman citizens. Who told you, then, that these are among the things in our own control, and not the affair of others? And who can give to another the things which he has not himself? "Well, but get them, then, that we too may have a share." If I can get them with the preservation of my own honor and fidelity and greatness of mind, show me the way and I will get them; but if you require me to lose my own proper good that you may gain what is not good, consider how inequitable and foolish you are. Besides, which would you rather have, a sum of money, or a friend of fidelity and honor? Rather assist me, then, to gain this character than require me to do those things by which I may lose

it. Well, but my country, say you, as far as depends on me, will be unassisted. Here again, what assistance is this you mean? "It will not have porticoes nor baths of your providing." And what signifies that? Why, neither does a smith provide it with shoes, or a shoemaker with arms. It is enough if everyone fully performs his own proper business. And were you to supply it with another citizen of honor and fidelity, would not he be of use to it? Yes. Therefore neither are you yourself useless to it. "What place, then, say you, will I hold in the state?" Whatever you can hold with the preservation of your fidelity and honor. But if, by desiring to be useful to that, you lose these, of what use can you be to your country when you are become faithless and void of shame.

25. Is anyone preferred before you at an entertainment, or in a compliment, or in being admitted to a consultation? If these things are good, you ought to be glad that he has gotten them; and if they are evil, don't be grieved that you have not gotten them. And remember that you cannot, without using the same means [which others do] to acquire things not in our own control, expect to be thought worthy of an equal share of them. For how can he who does not frequent the door of any [great] man, does not attend him, does not praise him, have an equal share with him who does? You are unjust, then, and insatiable, if you are unwilling to pay the price for which these things are sold, and would have them for nothing. For how much is lettuce sold? Fifty cents, for instance. If another, then, paying fifty cents, takes the lettuce, and you, not paying it, go without them, don't imagine that he has gained any advantage over you. For as he has the lettuce, so you have the fifty cents which you did not give. So, in the present case, you have not been invited to such a person's entertainment, because you have not paid him the price for which a supper is sold. It is sold for praise; it is sold for attendance. Give him then the value, if it is for your advantage. But if you would, at the same time, not pay the one and yet receive the other, you are insatiable, and a blockhead. Have you nothing, then, instead of the supper? Yes, indeed, you have: the not praising him, whom you don't like to praise; the not bearing with his behavior at coming in.

26. The will of nature may be learned from those things in

which we don't distinguish from each other. For example, when our neighbor's boy breaks a cup, or the like, we are presently ready to say, "These things will happen." Be assured, then, that when your own cup likewise is broken, you ought to be affected just as when another's cup was broken. Apply this in like manner to greater things. Is the child or wife of another dead? There is no one who would not say, "This is a human accident." but if anyone's own child happens to die, it is presently, "Alas I how wretched am I!" But it should be remembered how we are affected in hearing the same thing concerning others.

27. As a mark is not set up for the sake of missing the aim, so neither does the nature of evil exist in the world.

28. If a person gave your body to any stranger he met on his way, you would certainly be angry. And do you feel no shame in handing over your own mind to be confused and mystified by anyone who happens to verbally attack you?

29. In every affair consider what precedes and follows, and then undertake it. Otherwise you will begin with spirit; but not having thought of the consequences, when some of them appear you will shamefully desist. "I would conquer at the Olympic games." But consider what precedes and follows, and then, if it is for your advantage, engage in the affair. You must conform to rules, submit to a diet, refrain from dainties; exercise your body, whether you choose it or not, at a stated hour, in heat and cold; you must drink no cold water, nor sometimes even wine. In a word, you must give yourself up to your master, as to a physician. Then, in the combat, you may be thrown into a ditch, dislocate your arm, turn your ankle, swallow dust, be whipped, and, after all, lose the victory. When you have evaluated all this, if your inclination still holds, then go to war. Otherwise, take notice, you will behave like children who sometimes play like wrestlers, sometimes gladiators, sometimes blow a trumpet, and sometimes act a tragedy when they have seen and admired these shows. Thus you too will be at one time a wrestler, at another a gladiator, now a philosopher, then an orator; but with your whole soul, nothing at all. Like an ape, you mimic all you see, and one thing after another is sure to please you, but is out

of favor as soon as it becomes familiar. For you have never entered upon anything considerately, nor after having viewed the whole matter on all sides, or made any scrutiny into it, but rashly, and with a cold inclination. Thus some, when they have seen a philosopher and heard a man speaking like Euphrates (though, indeed, who can speak like him?), have a mind to be philosophers too. Consider first, man, what the matter is, and what your own nature is able to bear. If you would be a wrestler, consider your shoulders, your back, your thighs; for different persons are made for different things. Do you think that you can act as you do, and be a philosopher? That you can eat and drink, and be angry and discontented as you are now? You must watch, you must labor, you must get the better of certain appetites, must quit your acquaintance, be despised by your servant, be laughed at by those you meet; come off worse than others in everything, in magistracies, in honors, in courts of judicature. When you have considered all these things round, approach, if you please; if, by parting with them, you have a mind to purchase apathy, freedom, and tranquillity. If not, don't come here; don't, like children, be one while a philosopher, then a publican, then an orator, and then one of Caesar's officers. These things are not consistent. You must be one man, either good or bad. You must cultivate either your own ruling faculty or externals, and apply yourself either to things within or without you; that is, be either a philosopher, or one of the vulgar.

30. Duties are universally measured by relations. Is anyone a father? If so, it is implied that the children should take care of him, submit to him in everything, patiently listen to his reproaches, his correction. But he is a bad father. Is you naturally entitled, then, to a good father? No, only to a father. Is a brother unjust? Well, keep your own situation towards him. Consider not what he does, but what you are to do to keep your own faculty of choice in a state conformable to nature. For another will not hurt you unless you please. You will then be hurt when you think you are hurt. In this manner, therefore, you will find, from the idea of a neighbor, a citizen, a general, the corresponding duties if you accustom yourself to contemplate the several relations.

31. Be assured that the essential property of piety towards

the gods is to form right opinions concerning them, as existing "I and as governing the universe with goodness and justice. And fix yourself in this resolution, to obey them, and yield to them, and willingly follow them in all events, as produced by the most perfect understanding. For thus you will never find fault with the gods, nor accuse them as neglecting you. And it is not possible for this to be effected any other way than by withdrawing yourself from things not in our own control, and placing good or evil in those only which are. For if you suppose any of the things not in our own control to be either good or evil, when you are disappointed of what you wish, or incur what you would avoid, you must necessarily find fault with and blame the authors. For every animal is naturally formed to fly and abhor things that appear hurtful, and the causes of them; and to pursue and admire those which appear beneficial, and the causes of them. It is impractical, then, that one who supposes himself to be hurt should be happy about the person who, he thinks, hurts him, just as it is impossible to be happy about the hurt itself. Hence, also, a father is reviled by a son, when he does not impart to him the things which he takes to be good; and the supposing empire to be a good made Polynices and Eteocles mutually enemies. On this account the husbandman, the sailor, the merchant, on this account those who lose wives and children, revile the gods. For where interest is, there too is piety placed. So that, whoever is careful to regulate his desires and aversions as he ought, is, by the very same means, careful of piety likewise. But it is also incumbent on everyone to offer libations and sacrifices and first fruits, conformably to the customs of his country, with purity, and not in a slovenly manner, nor negligently, nor sparingly, nor beyond his ability.

32. When you have recourse to divination, remember that you know not what the event will be, and you come to learn it of the diviner; but of what nature it is you know before you come, at least if you are a philosopher. For if it is among the things not in our own control, it can by no means be either good or evil. Don't, therefore, bring either desire or aversion with you to the diviner (else you will approach him trembling), but first acquire a distinct knowledge that every event is indifferent and nothing to you., of whatever sort it may be, for it will be in your power

to make a right use of it, and this no one can hinder; then come with confidence to the gods, as your counselors, and afterwards, when any counsel is given you, remember what counselors you have assumed, and whose advice you will neglect if you disobey. Come to divination, as Socrates prescribed, in cases of which the whole consideration relates to the event, and in which no opportunities are afforded by reason, or any other art, to discover the thing proposed to be learned. When, therefore, it is our duty to share the danger of a friend or of our country, we ought not to consult the oracle whether we will share it with them or not. For, though the diviner should forewarn you that the victims are unfavorable, this means no more than that either death or mutilation or exile is portended. But we have reason within us, and it directs, even with these hazards, to the greater diviner, the Pythian god, who cast out of the temple the person who gave no assistance to his friend while another was murdering him.

33. Immediately prescribe some character and form of conduce to yourself, which you may keep both alone and in company.

Be for the most part silent, or speak merely what is necessary, and in few words. We may, however, enter, though sparingly, into discourse sometimes when occasion calls for it, but not on any of the common subjects, of gladiators, or horse races, or athletic champions, or feasts, the vulgar topics of conversation; but principally not of men, so as either to blame, or praise, or make comparisons. If you are able, then, by your own conversation bring over that of your company to proper subjects; but, if you happen to be taken among strangers, be silent.

Don't allow your laughter be much, nor on many occasions, nor profuse.

Avoid swearing, if possible, altogether; if not, as far as you are able.

Avoid public and vulgar entertainments; but, if ever an occasion calls you to them, keep your attention upon the stretch, that you may not imperceptibly slide into vulgar manners. For be assured that if a person be ever so sound himself, yet, if his companion be infected, he who converses with him will be infected likewise.

Provide things relating to the body no further than mere use; as meat, drink, clothing, house, family. But strike off and reject everything relating to show and delicacy.

As far as possible, before marriage, keep yourself pure from familiarities with women, and, if you indulge them, let it be lawfully." But don't therefore be troublesome and full of reproofs to those who use these liberties, nor frequently boast that you yourself don't.

If anyone tells you that such a person speaks ill of you, don't make excuses about what is said of you, but answer: " He does not know my other faults, else he would not have mentioned only these."

It is not necessary for you to appear often at public spectacles; but if ever there is a proper occasion for you to be there, don't appear more solicitous for anyone than for yourself; that is, wish things to be only just as they are, and him only to conquer who is the conqueror, for thus you will meet with no hindrance. But abstain entirely from declamations and derision and violent emotions. And when you come away, don't discourse a great deal on what has passed, and what does not contribute to your own amendment. For it would appear by such discourse that you were immoderately struck with the show.

Go not [of your own accord] to the rehearsals of any
 authors , nor appear [at them] readily. But, if you do appear, keep your gravity and sedateness, and at the same time avoid being morose.

When you are going to confer with anyone, and particularly of those in a superior station, represent to yourself how Socrates or Zeno would behave in such a case, and you will not be at a loss to make a proper use of whatever may occur.

When you are going to any of the people in power, represent

to yourself that you will not find him at home; that you will not be admitted; that the doors will not be opened to you; that he will take no notice of you. If, with all this, it is your duty to go, bear what happens, and never say [to yourself], " It was not worth so much." For this is vulgar, and like a man dazed by external things.

In parties of conversation, avoid a frequent and excessive mention of your own actions and dangers. For, however agreeable it may be to yourself to mention the risks you have run, it is not equally agreeable to others to hear your adventures. Avoid, likewise, an endeavor to excite laughter. For this is a slippery point, which may throw you into vulgar manners, and, besides, may be apt to lessen you in the esteem of your acquaintance. Approaches to indecent discourse are likewise dangerous. Whenever, therefore, anything of this sort happens, if there be a proper opportunity, rebuke him who makes advances that way; or, at least, by silence and blushing and a forbidding look, show yourself to be displeased by such talk.

34. If you are struck by the appearance of any promised pleasure, guard yourself against being hurried away by it; but let the affair wait your leisure, and procure yourself some delay. Then bring to your mind both points of time: that in which you will enjoy the pleasure, and that in which you will repent and reproach yourself after you have enjoyed it; and set before you, in opposition to these, how you will be glad and applaud yourself if you abstain. And even though it should appear to you a seasonable gratification, take heed that its enticing, and agreeable and attractive force may not subdue you; but set in opposition to this how much better it is to be conscious of having gained so great a victory.

35. When you do anything from a clear judgment that it ought to be done, never shun the being seen to do it, even though the world should make a wrong supposition about it; for, if you don't act right, shun the action itself; but, if you do, why are you afraid of those who censure you wrongly?

36. As the proposition, "Either it is day or it is night," is

extremely proper for a disjunctive argument, but quite improper in a conjunctive one, so, at a feast, to choose the largest share is very suitable to the bodily appetite, but utterly inconsistent with the social spirit of an entertainment. When you eat with another, then, remember not only the value of those things which are set before you to the body, but the value of that behavior which ought to be observed towards the person who gives the entertainment.

37. If you have assumed any character above your strength, you have both made an ill figure in that and quitted one which you might have supported.

38. When walking, you are careful not to step on a nail or turn your foot; so likewise be careful not to hurt the ruling faculty of your mind. And, if we were to guard against this in every action, we should undertake the action with the greater safety.

39. The body is to everyone the measure of the possessions proper for it, just as the foot is of the shoe. If, therefore, you stop at this, you will keep the measure; but if you move beyond it, you must necessarily be carried forward, as down a cliff; as in the case of a shoe, if you go beyond its fitness to the foot, it comes first to be gilded, then purple, and then studded with jewels. For to that which once exceeds a due measure, there is no bound.

40. Women from fourteen years old are flattered with the title of "mistresses" by the men. Therefore, perceiving that they are regarded only as qualified to give the men pleasure, they begin to adorn themselves, and in that to place ill their hopes. We should, therefore, fix our attention on making them sensible that they are valued for the appearance of decent, modest and discreet behavior.

41. It is a mark of want of genius to spend much time in things relating to the body, as to be long in our exercises, in eating and drinking, and in the discharge of other animal functions. These should be done incidentally and slightly, and our whole attention be engaged in the care of the understanding.

42. When any person harms you, or speaks badly of you, remember that he acts or speaks from a supposition of its being his duty. Now, it is not possible that he should follow what appears right to you, but what appears so to himself. Therefore, if he judges from a wrong appearance, he is the person hurt, since he too is the person deceived. For if anyone should suppose a true proposition to be false, the proposition is not hurt, but he who is deceived about it. Setting out, then, from these principles, you will meekly bear a person who reviles you, for you will say upon every occasion, "It seemed so to him."

43. Everything has two handles, the one by which it may be carried, the other by which it cannot. If your brother acts unjustly, don't lay hold on the action by the handle of his injustice, for by that it cannot be carried; but by the opposite, that he is your brother, that he was brought up with you; and thus you will lay hold on it, as it is to be carried.

44. These reasonings are unconnected: "I am richer than you, therefore I am better"; "I am more eloquent than you, therefore I am better." The connection is rather this: "I am richer than you, therefore my property is greater than yours;" "I am more eloquent than you, therefore my style is better than yours." But you, after all, are neither property nor style.

45. Does anyone bathe in a mighty little time? Don't say that he does it ill, but in a mighty little time. Does anyone drink a great quantity of wine? Don't say that he does ill, but that he drinks a great quantity. For, unless you perfectly understand the principle from which anyone acts, how should you know if he acts ill? Thus you will not run the hazard of assenting to any appearances but such as you fully comprehend.

46. Never call yourself a philosopher, nor talk a great deal among the unlearned about theorems, but act conformably to them. Thus, at an entertainment, don't talk how persons ought to eat, but eat as you ought. For remember that in this manner Socrates also universally avoided all ostentation. And when persons came to him and desired to be recommended by him to philosophers, he took and- recommended them, so well did he

bear being overlooked. So that if ever any talk should happen among the unlearned concerning philosophic theorems, be you, for the most part, silent. For there is great danger in immediately throwing out what you have not digested. And, if anyone tells you that you know nothing, and you are not nettled at it, then you may be sure that you have begun your business. For sheep don't throw up the grass to show the shepherds how much they have eaten; but, inwardly digesting their food, they outwardly produce wool and milk. Thus, therefore, do you likewise not show theorems to the unlearned, but the actions produced by them after they have been digested.

47. When you have brought yourself to supply the necessities of your body at a small price, don't pique yourself upon it; nor, if you drink water, be saying upon every occasion, "I drink water." But first consider how much more sparing and patient of hardship the poor are than we. But if at any time you would inure yourself by exercise to labor, and bearing hard trials, do it for your own sake, and not for the world; don't grasp statues, but, when you are violently thirsty, take a little cold water in your mouth, and spurt it out and tell nobody.

48. The condition and characteristic of a vulgar person, is, that he never expects either benefit or hurt from himself, but from externals. The condition and characteristic of a philosopher is, that he expects all hurt and benefit from himself. The marks of a proficient are, that he censures no one, praises no one, blames no one, accuses no one, says nothing concerning himself as being anybody, or knowing anything: when he is, in any instance, hindered or restrained, he accuses himself; and, if he is praised, he secretly laughs at the person who praises him; and, if he is censured, he makes no defense. But he goes about with the caution of sick or injured people, dreading to move anything that is set right, before it is perfectly fixed. He suppresses all desire in himself; he transfers his aversion to those things only which thwart the proper use of our own faculty of choice; the exertion of his active powers towards anything is very gentle; if he appears stupid or ignorant, he does not care, and, in a word, he watches himself as an enemy, and one in ambush.

49. When anyone shows himself overly confident in ability to understand and interpret the works of Chrysippus, say to yourself, " Unless Chrysippus had written obscurely, this person would have had no subject for his vanity. But what do I desire? To understand nature and follow her. I ask, then, who interprets her, and, finding Chrysippus does, I have recourse to him. I don't understand his writings. I seek, therefore, one to interpret them." So far there is nothing to value myself upon. And when I find an interpreter, what remains is to make use of his instructions. This alone is the valuable thing. But, if I admire nothing but merely the interpretation, what do I become more than a grammarian instead of a philosopher? Except, indeed, that instead of Homer I interpret Chrysippus. When anyone, therefore, desires me to read Chrysippus to him, I rather blush when I cannot show my actions agreeable and consonant to his discourse.

50. Whatever moral rules you have deliberately proposed to yourself. abide by them as they were laws, and as if you would be guilty of impiety by violating any of them. Don't regard what anyone says of you, for this, after all, is no concern of yours. How long, then, will you put off thinking yourself worthy of the highest improvements and follow the distinctions of reason? You have received the philosophical theorems, with which you ought to be familiar, and you have been familiar with them. What other master, then, do you wait for, to throw upon that the delay of reforming yourself? You are no longer a boy, but a grown man. If, therefore, you will be negligent and slothful, and always add procrastination to procrastination, purpose to purpose, and fix day after day in which you will attend to yourself, you will insensibly continue without proficiency, and, living and dying, persevere in being one of the vulgar. This instant, then, think yourself worthy of living as a man grown up, and a proficient. Let whatever appears to be the best be to you an inviolable law. And if any instance of pain or pleasure, or glory or disgrace, is set before you, remember that now is the combat, now the Olympiad comes on, nor can it be put off. By once being defeated and giving way, proficiency is lost, or by the contrary preserved. Thus Socrates became perfect, improving himself by everything. attending to nothing but reason. And though you are not yet a Socrates, you ought, however, to live as one desirous of becoming a Socrates.

51. The first and most necessary topic in philosophy is that of the use of moral theorems, such as, "We ought not to lie;" the second is that of demonstrations, such as, "What is the origin of our obligation not to lie;" the third gives strength and articulation to the other two, such as, "What is the origin of this is a demonstration." For what is demonstration? What is consequence? What contradiction? What truth? What falsehood? The third topic, then, is necessary on the account of the second, and the second on the account of the first. But the most necessary, and that whereon we ought to rest, is the first. But we act just on the contrary. For we spend all our time on the third topic, and employ all our diligence about that, and entirely neglect the first. Therefore, at the same time that we lie, we are immediately prepared to show how it is demonstrated that lying is not right.

52. Upon all occasions we ought to have these maxims ready at hand:

"Conduct me, Jove, and you, o Destiny,
Wherever your decrees have fixed my station."
Cleanthes

"I follow cheerfully; and, did I not,
Wicked and wretched, I must follow still
Whoever yields properly to Fate, is deemed
Wise among men, and knows the laws of heaven."
Euripides, Frag. 965

And this third:

"o Crito, if it thus pleases the gods, thus let it be. Anytus and Melitus may kill me indeed, but hurt me they cannot."
Plato's Crito and Apology

THE END

THE DISCOURSES

OF THE THINGS WHICH ARE IN OUR POWER AND NOT IN OUR POWER.—Of all the faculties (except that which I shall soon mention), you will find not one which is capable of contemplating itself, and, consequently, not capable either of approving or disapproving. How far does the grammatic art possess the contemplating power? As far as forming a judgment about what is written and spoken. And how far music? As far as judging about melody. Does either of them then contemplate itself? By no means. But when you must write something to your friend, grammar will tell you what words you should write; but whether you should write or not, grammar will not tell you. And so it is with music as to musical sounds; but whether you should sing at the present time and play on the lute, or do neither, music will not tell you. What faculty then will tell you? That which contemplates both itself and all other things. And what is this faculty? The rational faculty; for this is the only faculty that we have received which examines itself, what it is, and what power it has, and what is the value of this gift, and examines all other faculties: for what else is there which tells us that golden things are beautiful, for they do not say so themselves? Evidently it is the faculty which is capable of judging of appearances. What else judges of music, grammar, and the other faculties, proves their uses, and points out the occasions for using them? Nothing else.

What then should a man have in readiness in such circumstances? What else than this? What is mine, and what is not mine; and what is permitted to me, and what is not permitted to me. I must die. Must I then die lamenting? I must be put in chains. Must I then also lament? I must go into exile. Does any man then hinder me from going with smiles and cheerfulness and contentment? Tell me the secret which you possess. I will not, for this is in my power. But I will put you in chains. Man, what are you talking about? Me, in chains? You may fetter my leg, but my will not even Zeus himself can overpower. I will throw you into prison. My poor body, you mean. I will cut your head off. When then have I told you that my head alone cannot be cut off? These are the things which philosophers should meditate on, which they should write daily, in which they should exercise themselves.

What then did Agrippinus say? He said, "I am not a hindrance to myself." When it was reported to him that his trial was going on in the Senate, he said: "I hope it may turn out well; but it is the fifth hour of the day"—this was the time when he was used to exercise himself and then take the cold bath,—"let us go and take our exercise." After he had taken his exercise, one comes and tells him, "You have been condemned." "To banishment," he replies, "or to death?" "To banishment." "What about my property?" "It is not taken from you." "Let us go to Aricia then," he said, "and dine."

HOW A MAN ON EVERY OCCASION CAN MAINTAIN HIS PROPER CHARACTER.—To the rational animal only is the irrational intolerable; but that which is rational is tolerable. Blows are not naturally intolerable. How is that? See how the Lacedaemonians endure whipping when they have learned that whipping is consistent with reason. To hang yourself is not intolerable. When then you have the opinion that it is rational, you go and hang yourself. In short, if we observe, we shall find that the animal man is pained by nothing so much as by that which is irrational; and, on the contrary, attracted to nothing so much as to that which is rational.

Only consider at what price you sell your own will: if for no other reason, at least for this, that you sell it not for a small sum. But that which is great and superior perhaps belongs to Socrates and such as are like him. Why then, if we are naturally such, are not a very great number of us like him? Is it true then that all horses become swift, that all dogs are skilled in tracking footprints? What then, since I am naturally dull, shall I, for this reason, take no pains? I hope not. Epictetus is not superior to Socrates; but if he is not inferior, this is enough for me; for I shall never be a Milo, and yet I do not neglect my body; nor shall I be a Croesus, and yet I do not neglect my property; nor, in a word, do we neglect looking after anything because we despair of reaching the highest degree.

HOW A MAN SHOULD PROCEED FROM THE PRINCIPLE OF GOD BEING THE FATHER OF ALL MEN TO THE REST.—If a man should be able to assent to this doctrine as he ought, that we are all sprung from God in an especial manner, and that God is the father both of men and of gods, I suppose that he would never have any ignoble or mean thoughts about himself. But if Cæsar (the emperor) should adopt you, no one could endure your arrogance; and if you know that you are the son of Zeus, will you not be elated? Yet we do not so; but since these two things are mingled in the generation of man, body in common with the animals, and reason and intelligence in common with the gods, many incline to this kinship, which is miserable and mortal; and some few to that which is divine and happy. Since then it is of necessity that every man uses everything according to the opinion which he has about it, those, the few, who think that they are formed for fidelity and modesty and a sure use of appearances have no mean or ignoble thoughts about themselves; but with the many it is quite the contrary. For they say, What am I? A poor, miserable man, with my wretched bit of flesh. Wretched, indeed; but you possess something better than your bit of flesh. Why then do you neglect that which is better, and why do you attach yourself to this?

Through this kinship with the flesh, some of us inclining to it become like wolves, faithless and treacherous and mischievous; some become like lions, savage and bestial and untamed; but the greater part of us become foxes, and other worse animals. For what else is a slanderer and malignant man than a fox, or some other more wretched and meaner animal? See then and take care that you do not become some one of these miserable things.

OF PROGRESS OR IMPROVEMENT.—He who is making progress, having learned from philosophers that desire means the desire of good things, and aversion means aversion from bad things; having learned too that happiness and tranquillity are not attainable by man otherwise than by not failing to obtain what he desires, and not falling into that which he would avoid; such a man takes from himself desire altogether and confers it, but he employs his aversion only on things which are dependent on his will. For if he attempts to avoid anything independent of his will, he knows that sometimes he will fall in with something which he wishes to avoid, and he will be unhappy. Now if virtue promises good fortune and tranquillity and happiness, certainly also the progress towards virtue is progress towards each of these things. For it is always true that to whatever point the perfecting of anything leads us, progress is an approach towards this point.

How then do we admit that virtue is such as I have said, and yet seek progress in other things and make a display of it? What is the product of virtue? Tranquillity. Who then makes improvement? Is it he who has read many books of Chrysippus? But does virtue consist in having understood Chrysippus? If this is so, progress is clearly nothing else than knowing a great deal of Chrysippus. But now we admit that virtue produces one thing, and we declare that approaching near to it is another thing, namely, progress or improvement. Such a person, says one, is already able to read Chrysippus by himself. Indeed, sir, you are making great progress. What kind of progress? But why do you mock the man? Why do you draw him away from the perception of his own misfortunes? Will you not show him the effect of virtue that he may learn where to look for improvement? Seek it there, wretch, where your work lies. And where is your work? In desire and in aversion, that you may not be disappointed in your desire, and that you may not fall into that which you would avoid; in your pursuit and avoiding, that you commit no error; in assent and suspension of assent, that you be not deceived. The first things, and the most necessary are those which I have named. But if with trembling and lamentation you seek not to fall into that which you avoid, tell me how you are improving.

Do you then show me your improvement in these things? If I were talking to an athlete, I should say, Show me your shoulders; and then he might say, Here are my Halteres. You and your

Halteres look to that. I should reply, I wish to see the effect of the Halteres. So, when you say: Take the treatise on the active powers ([Greek: hormea]), and see how I have studied it, I reply: Slave, I am not inquiring about this, but how you exercise pursuit and avoidance, desire and aversion, how you design and purpose and prepare yourself, whether conformably to nature or not. If conformably, give me evidence of it, and I will say that you are making progress; but if not conformably, be gone, and not only expound your books, but write such books yourself; and what will you gain by it? Do you not know that the whole book costs only five denarii? Does then the expounder seem to be worth more than five denarii? Never then look for the matter itself in one place, and progress towards it in another. Where then is progress? If any of you, withdrawing himself from externals, turns to his own will ([Greek: proairesis]) to exercise it and to improve it by labor, so as to make it conformable to nature, elevated, free, unrestrained, unimpeded, faithful, modest; and if he has learned that he who desires or avoids the things which are not in his power can neither be faithful nor free, but of necessity he must change with them and be tossed about with them as in a tempest, and of necessity must subject himself to others who have the power to procure or prevent what lie desires or would avoid; finally, when he rises in the morning, if he observes and keeps these rules, bathes as a man of fidelity, eats as a modest man; in like manner, if in every matter that occurs he works out his chief principles ([Greek: ta proaegoumena]) as the runner does with reference to running, and the trainer of the voice with reference to the voice—this is the man who truly makes progress, and this is the man who has not travelled in vain. But if he has strained his efforts to the practice of reading books, and labors only at this, and has travelled for this, I tell him to return home immediately, and not to neglect his affairs there; for this for which he has travelled is nothing. But the other thing is something, to study how a man can rid his life of lamentation and groaning, and saying, Woe to me, and wretched that I am, and to rid it also of misfortune and disappointment, and to learn what death is, and exile, and prison, and poison, that he may be able to say when he is in fetters, Dear Crito, if it is the will of the gods that it be so, let it be so; and not to say, Wretched am I, an old man: have I kept my gray hairs for this? Who is it that speaks thus? Do you think that I shall name some man of no repute and of low condition? Does not Priam say this? Does not Oedipus say this? Nay, all kings say it! For what else is tragedy than the perturbations ([Greek: pathae]) of men who value externals exhibited in this kind of poetry? But if a man must learn by fiction that no external things which are independent of the will concern us, for my part I should like this fiction, by the aid of which I should live happily and undisturbed. But you must consider for yourselves what you wish.

What then does Chrysippus teach us? The reply is, to know that these things are not false, from which happiness comes and tranquillity arises. Take my books, and you will learn how true and conformable to nature are the things which make me free from perturbations. O great good fortune! O the great benefactor who points out the way! To Triptolemus all men have erected temples and altars, because he gave us food by cultivation; but to him who discovered truth and brought it to light and communicated it to all, not the truth which shows us how to live, but how to live well, who of you for this reason has built an altar, or a temple, or has dedicated a statue, or who worships God for this? Because the gods have given the vine, or wheat, we sacrifice to them; but because they have produced in the human mind that fruit by which they designed to show us the truth which relates to happiness, shall we not thank God for this?

AGAINST THE ACADEMICS.—If a man, said Epictetus, opposes evident truths, it is not easy to find arguments by which we shall make him change his opinion. But this does not arise either from the man's strength or the teacher's weakness; for when the man, though he has been confuted, is hardened like a stone, how shall we then be able to deal with him by argument?

Now there are two kinds of hardening, one of the understanding, the other of the sense of shame, when a man is resolved not to assent to what is manifest nor to desist from contradictions. Most of us are afraid of mortification of the body, and would contrive all means to avoid such a thing, but we care not about the soul's mortification. And indeed with regard to the soul, if a man be in such a state as not to apprehend anything, or understand at all, we think that he is in a bad condition; but if the sense of shame and modesty are deadened, this we call even power (or strength).

OF PROVIDENCE.—From everything, which is or happens in the world, it is easy to praise Providence, if a man possesses these two qualities: the faculty of seeing what belongs and happens to all persons and things, and a grateful disposition. If he does not possess these two qualities, one man will not see the use of things which are and which happen: another will not be thankful for them, even if he does know them. If God had made colors, but had not made the faculty of seeing them, what would have been their use? None at all. On the other hand, if he had made the faculty of vision, but had not made objects such as to fall under the faculty, what in that case also would have been the use of it? None at all. Well, suppose that he had made both, but had not made light? In that case, also, they would have been of no use. Who is it then who has fitted this to that and that to this?

What, then, are these things done in us only? Many, indeed, in us only, of which the rational animal had peculiar need; but you will find many common to us with irrational animals. Do they then understand what is done? By no means. For use is one thing, and understanding is another; God had need of irrational animals to make use of appearances, but of us to understand the use of appearances. It is therefore enough for them to eat and to drink, and to copulate, and to do all the other things which they severally do. But for us, to whom he has given also the intellectual faculty, these things are not sufficient; for unless we act in a proper and orderly manner, and conformably to the nature and constitution of each thing, we shall never attain our true end. For where the constitutions of living beings are different, there also the acts and the ends are different. In those animals then whose constitution is adapted only to use, use alone is enough; but in an animal (man), which has also the power of understanding the use, unless there be the due exercise of the understanding, he will never attain his proper end. Well then God constitutes every animal, one to be eaten, another to serve for agriculture, another to supply cheese, and another for some like use; for which purposes what need is there to understand appearances and to be able to distinguish them? But God has introduced man to be a spectator of God and of his works; and not only a spectator of them, but an interpreter. For this reason it is shameful for man to begin and to end where irrational animals do; but rather he ought to begin where they begin, and to end where nature ends in us; and nature ends in contemplation and understanding, and in a way of life conformable to nature. Take care then not to die without having been spectators of these things.

But you take a journey to Olympia to see the work of Phidias, and all of you think it a misfortune to die without having seen such things. But when there is no need to take a journey, and where a man is, there he has the works (of God) before him, will you not desire to see and understand them? Will you not perceive either what you are, or what you were born for, or what this is for which you have received the faculty of sight? But you may say, There are some things disagreeable and troublesome in life. And are there none at Olympia? Are you not scorched? Are you not pressed by a crowd? Are you not without comfortable means of bathing? Are you not wet when it rains? Have you not abundance of noise, clamor, and other disagreeable things? But I suppose that setting all these things off against the magnificence of the spectacle, you bear and endure. Well then and have you not received faculties by which you will be able to bear all that happens? Have you not received greatness of soul? Have you not received manliness? Have you not received endurance? And why do I trouble myself about anything that can happen if I possess greatness of soul? What shall distract my mind, or disturb me, or appear painful? Shall I not use the power for the purposes for which I received it, and shall I grieve and lament over what happens?

Come, then, do you also having observed these things look to the faculties which you have, and when you have looked at them, say: Bring now, O Zeus, any difficulty that thou pleasest, for I have means given to me by thee and powers for honoring myself through the things which happen. You do not so; but you sit still, trembling for fear that some things will happen, and weeping, and lamenting, and groaning for what does happen; and then you blame the gods. For what is the consequence of such meanness of spirit but impiety? And yet God has not only given us these faculties, by which we shall be able to bear everything that happens without being depressed or broken by it; but, like a good king and a true father, He has given us these faculties free from hindrance, subject to no compulsion, unimpeded, and has put them entirely in our own power, without even having reserved to Himself any power of hindering or impeding. You, who have received these powers free and as your own, use them not; you do not even see what you have received, and from whom; some of you being blinded to the giver, and not even acknowledging your benefactor, and others, through meanness of spirit, betaking yourselves to fault-finding and making charges against God. Yet I will show to you that you have powers and means for greatness of soul and manliness; but what powers you have for finding fault making accusations, do you show me.

HOW FROM THE FACT THAT WE ARE AKIN TO GOD A MAN MAY PROCEED TO THE CONSEQUENCES.—I indeed think that the old man ought to be sitting here, not to contrive how you may have no mean thoughts nor mean and ignoble talk about yourselves, but to take care that there be not among us any young men of such a mind, that when they have recognized their kinship to God, and that we are fettered by these bonds, the body, I mean, and its possessions, and whatever else on account of them is necessary to us for the economy and commerce of life, they should intend to throw off these things as if they were burdens painful and intolerable, and to depart to their kinsmen. But this is the labor that your teacher and instructor ought to be employed upon, if he really were what he should be. You should come to him and say: Epictetus, we can no longer endure being bound to this poor body, and feeding it, and giving it drink and rest, and cleaning it, and for the sake of the body complying with the wishes of these and of those. Are not these things indifferent and nothing to us; and is not death no evil? And are we not in a manner kinsmen of God, and did we not come from him? Allow us to depart to the place from which we came; allow us to be released at last from these bonds by which we are bound and weighed down. Here there are robbers and thieves and courts of justice, and those who are named tyrants, and think that they have some power over us by means of the body and its possessions. Permit us to show them that they have no power over any man. And I on my part would say: Friends, wait for God: when he shall give the signal and release you from this service, then go to him; but for the present endure to dwell in this place where he has put you. Short indeed is this time of your dwelling here, and easy to bear for those who are so disposed; for what tyrant, or what thief, or what courts of justice are formidable to those who have thus considered as things of no value the body and the possessions of the body? Wait then, do not depart without a reason.

OF CONTENTMENT.—With respect to gods, there are some who say that a divine being does not exist; others say that it exists, but is inactive and careless, and takes no forethought about anything; a third class say that such a being exists and exercises forethought, but only about great things and heavenly things, and about nothing on the earth; a fourth class say that a divine being exercises forethought both about things on the earth and heavenly things, but in a general way only, and not about things severally. There is a fifth class to whom Ulysses and Socrates belong, who say:

I move not without thy knowledge.—Iliad, x., 278.

Before all other things then it is necessary to inquire about each of these opinions, whether it is affirmed truly or not truly. For if there are no gods, how is it our proper end to follow them? And if they exist, but take no care of anything, in this case also how will it be right to follow them? But if indeed they do exist and look after things, still if there is nothing communicated from them to men, nor in fact to myself, how even so is it right (to follow them)? The wise and good man then, after considering all these things, submits his own mind to him who administers the whole, as good citizens do to the law of the state. He who is receiving instruction ought to come to be instructed with this intention, How shall I follow the gods in all things, how shall I be contented with the divine administration, and how can I become free? For he is free to whom everything happens according to his will, and whom no man can hinder. What then, is freedom madness? Certainly not; for madness and freedom do not consist.

But, you say, I would have everything result just as I like, and in whatever way I like. You are mad, you are beside yourself. Do you not know that freedom is a noble and valuable thing? But for me inconsiderately to wish for things to happen as I inconsiderately like, this appears to be not only not noble, but even most base. For how do we proceed in the matter of writing? Do I wish to write the name of Dion as I choose? No, but I am taught to choose to write it as it ought to be written. And how with respect to music? In the same manner. And what universally in every art or science? Just the same. If it were not so, it would be of no value to know anything, if knowledge were adapted to every man's whim. Is it then in this alone, in this which is the greatest and the chief thing, I mean freedom, that I am permitted to will inconsiderately? By no means; but to be instructed is this, to learn to wish that everything may happen as it does. And how do things happen? As the disposer has disposed them? And he has appointed summer and winter, and abundance and scarcity, and virtue and vice, and all such opposites for the harmony of the whole; and to each of us he has given a body, and parts of the body, and possessions, and companions.

What then remains, or what method is discovered of holding commerce with them? Is there such a method by which they shall do what seems fit to them, and we not the less shall be in a mood which is conformable to nature? But you are unwilling to endure, and are discontented; and if you are alone, you call it solitude; and if you are with men, you call them knaves and robbers; and you find fault with your own parents and children, and brothers and neighbors. But you ought when you are alone to call this condition by the name of tranquillity and freedom, and to think yourself like to the gods; and when you are with many, you ought not to call it crowd, nor trouble, nor uneasiness, but festival and assembly, and so accept all contentedly.

What then is the punishment of those who do not accept? It is to be what they are. Is any person dissatisfied with being alone? Let him be alone. Is a man dissatisfied with his parents? Let him be a bad son, and lament. Is he dissatisfied with his children? Let him be a bad father. Cast him into prison. What prison? Where he is already, for he is there against his will; and where a man is against his will, there he is in prison. So Socrates was not in prison, for he was there willingly. Must my leg then be lamed? Wretch, do you then on account of one poor leg find fault with the world? Will you not willingly surrender it for the whole? Will you not withdraw from it? Will you not gladly part with it to him who gave it? And will you be vexed and discontented with the things established by Zeus, which he, with the Moirae (fates) who were present and spinning the thread of your generation, defined and put in order? Know you not how small a part you are compared with the whole. I mean with respect to the body, for as to intelligence you are not inferior to the gods nor less; for the magnitude of intelligence is not measured by length nor yet by height, but by thoughts.

HOW EVERYTHING MAY BE DONE ACCEPTABLY TO THE GODS.—When some one asked, How may a man eat acceptably to the gods, he answered: If he can eat justly and contentedly, and with equanimity, and temperately, and orderly, will it not be also acceptable to the gods? But when you have asked for warm water and the slave has not heard, or if he did hear has brought only tepid water, or he is not even found to be in the house, then not to be vexed or to burst with passion, is not this acceptable to the gods? How then shall a man endure such persons as this slave? Slave yourself, will you not bear with your own brother, who has Zeus for his progenitor, and is like a son from the same seeds and of the same descent from above? But if you have been put in any such higher place, will you immediately make yourself a tyrant? Will you not remember who you are, and whom you rule? That they are kinsmen, that they are brethren by nature, that they are the offspring of Zeus? But I have purchased them, and they have not purchased me. Do you see in what direction you are looking, that it is towards the earth, towards the pit, that it is towards these wretched laws of dead men? but towards the laws of the gods you are not looking.

WHAT PHILOSOPHY PROMISES.—When a man was consulting him how he should persuade his brother to cease being angry with him, Epictetus replied: Philosophy does not propose to secure for a man any external thing. If it did (or if it were not, as I say), philosophy would be allowing something which is not within its province. For as the carpenter's material is wood, and that of the statuary is copper, so the matter of the art of living is each man's life. When then is my brother's? That again belongs to his own art; but with respect to yours, it is one of the external things, like a piece of land, like health, like reputation. But Philosophy promises none of these. In every circumstance I will maintain, she says, the governing part conformable to nature. Whose governing part? His in whom I am, she says.

How then shall my brother cease to be angry with me? Bring him to me and I will tell him. But I have nothing to say to you about his anger.

When the man who was consulting him said, I seek to know this, How, even if my brother is not reconciled to me, shall I maintain myself in a state conformable to nature? Nothing great, said Epictetus, is produced suddenly, since not even the grape or the fig is. If you say to me now that you want a fig, I will answer to you that it requires time: let it flower first, then put forth fruit, and then ripen. Is then the fruit of a fig-tree not perfected suddenly and in one hour, and would you possess the fruit of a man's mind in so short a time and so easily? Do not expect it, even if I tell you.

THAT WE OUGHT NOT TO BE ANGRY WITH THE ERRORS (FAULTS) OF OTHERS.—Ought not then this robber and this adulterer to be destroyed? By no means say so, but speak rather in this way: This man who has been mistaken and deceived about the most important things, and blinded, not in the faculty of vision which distinguishes white and black, but in the faculty which distinguishes good and bad, should we not destroy him? If you speak thus you will see how inhuman this is which you say, and that it is just as if you would say, Ought we not to destroy this blind and deaf man? But if the greatest harm is the privation of the greatest things, and the greatest thing in every man is the will or choice such as it ought to be, and a man is deprived of this will, why are you also angry with him? Man, you ought not to be affected contrary to nature by the bad things of another. Pity him rather; drop this readiness to be offended and to hate, and these words which the many utter:

"These accursed and odious fellows." How have you been made so wise at once? and how are you so peevish? Why then are we angry? Is it because we value so much the things of which these men rob us? Do not admire your clothes, and then you will not be angry with the thief. Consider this matter thus: you have fine clothes; your neighbor has not; you have a window; you wish to air the clothes. The thief does not know wherein man's good consists, but he thinks that it consist in having fine clothes, the very thing which you also think. Must he not then come and take them away? When you show a cake to greedy persons, and swallow it all yourself, do you expect them not to snatch it from you? Do not provoke them; do not have a window; do not air your clothes. I also lately had an iron lamp placed by the side of my household gods; hearing a noise at the door, I ran down, and found that the lamp had been carried off. I reflected that he who had taken the lamp had done nothing strange. What then? To-morrow, I said, you will find an earthen lamp; for a man only loses that which he has. I have lost my garment. The reason is that you had a garment. I have a pain in my head. Have you any pain in your horns? Why then are you troubled? For we only lose those things, we have only pains about those things, which we possess.

But the tyrant will chain—what? The leg. He will take away—what? The neck. What then will he not chain and not take away? The will. This is why the ancients taught the maxim, Know thyself. Therefore we ought to exercise ourselves in small things, and beginning with them to proceed to the greater. I have pain in the head. Do not say, Alas! I have pain in the ear. Do not say alas! And I do not say that you are not allowed to groan, but do not groan inwardly; and if your slave is slow in bringing a bandage, do not cry out and torment yourself, and say, Every body hates me; for who would not hate such a man? For the future, relying on these opinions, walk about upright, free; not trusting to the size of your body, as an athlete, for a man ought not to be invincible in the way that an ass is.

HOW WE SHOULD BEHAVE TO TYRANTS.—If a man possesses any superiority, or thinks that he does when he does not, such a man, if he is uninstructed, will of necessity be puffed up through it. For instance, the tyrant says, I am master of all! And what can you do for me? Can you give me desire which shall have no hindrance? How can you? Have you the infallible power of avoiding what you would avoid? Have you the power of moving towards an object without error? And how do you possess this power? Come, when you are in a ship, do you trust to yourself or to the helmsman? And when you are in a chariot, to whom do you trust but to the driver? And how is it in all other arts? Just the same. In what, then, lies your power? All men pay respect to me. Well, I also pay respect to my platter, and I wash it and wipe it; and for the sake of my oil-flask, I drive a peg into the wall. Well, then, are these things superior to me? No, but they supply some of my wants, and for this reason I take care of them. Well, do I not attend to my ass? Do I not wash his feet? Do I not clean him? Do you not know that every man has regard to himself, and to you just the same as he has regard to his ass? For who has regard to you as a man? Show me. Who wishes to become like you? Who imitates you, as he imitates Socrates? But I can cut off your head. You say right. I had forgotten that I must have regard to you, as I would to a fever and the bile, and raise an altar to you, as there is at Rome an altar to fever.

What is it then that disturbs and terrifies the multitude? Is it the tyrant and his guards? (By no means.) I hope that it is not so. It is not possible that what is by nature free can be disturbed by anything else, or hindered by any other thing than by itself. But it is a man's own opinions which disturb him. For when the tyrant says to a man, I will chain your leg, he who values his leg says, Do not; have pity. But he who values his own will says, If it appears more advantageous to you, chain it. Do you not care? I do not care. I will show you that I am master. You cannot do that. Zeus has set me free; do you think that he intended to allow his own son to be enslaved? But you are master of my carcase; take it. So when you approach me, you have no regard to me? No, but I have regard to myself; and if you wish me to say that I have regard to you also, I tell you that I have the same regard to you that I have to my pipkin.

What then? When absurd notions about things independent of our will, as if they were good and (or) bad, lie at the bottom of our opinions, we must of necessity pay regard to tyrants: for I wish that men would pay regard to tyrants only, and not also to the bedchamber men. How is it that the man becomes all at once wise, when Cæsar has made him superintendent of the close stool? How is it that we say immediately, Felicion spoke sensibly to me? I wish he were ejected from the bedchamber, that he might again appear to you to be a fool.

Has a man been exalted to the tribuneship? All who meet him offer their congratulations; one kisses his eyes, another the neck, and the slaves kiss his hands. He goes to his house, he finds torches lighted. He ascends the Capitol; he offers a sacrifice on the occasion. Now who ever sacrificed for having had good desires? for having acted conformably to nature? For in fact we thank the gods for those things in which we place our good.

A person was talking to me to-day about the priesthood of Augustus. I say to him: Man, let the thing alone; you will spend much for no purpose. But he replies, Those who draw up agreements will write my name. Do you then stand by those who read them, and say to such persons, It is I whose name is written there? And if you can now be present on ail such occasions, what will you do when you are dead? My name will remain. Write it on a stone, and it will remain. But come, what remembrance of you will there be beyond Nicopolis? But I shall wear a crown of gold. If you desire a crown at all, take a crown of roses and put it on, for it will be more elegant in appearance.

AGAINST THOSE WHO WISH TO BE ADMIRED.—When a man holds his proper station in life, he does not gape after things beyond it. Man, what do you wish to happen to you? I am satisfied if I desire and avoid conformably to nature, if I employ movements towards and from an object as I am by nature formed to do, and purpose and design and assent. Why then do you strut before us as if you had swallowed a spit? My wish has always been that those who meet me should admire me, and those who follow me should exclaim, O the great philosopher! Who are they by whom you wish to be admired? Are they not those of whom you are used to say that they are mad? Well, then, do you wish to be admired by madmen?

ON PRÆCOGNITIONS.—Præcognitions are common to all men, and præcognition is not contradictory to præcognition. For who of us does not assume that Good is useful and eligible, and in all circumstances that we ought to follow and pursue it? And who of us does not assume that Justice is beautiful and becoming? When then does the contradiction arise? It arises in the adaptation of the præcognitions to the particular cases. When one man says, "He has done well; he is a brave man," and another says, "Not so; but he has acted foolishly," then the disputes arise among men. This is the dispute among the Jews and the Syrians and the Egyptians and the Romans; not whether holiness should be preferred to all things and in all cases should be pursued, but whether it is holy to eat pig's flesh or not holy. You will find this dispute also between Agamemnon and Achilles; for call them forth. What do you say, Agamemnon? ought not that to be done which is proper and right? "Certainly." Well, what do you say, Achilles? do you not admit that what is good ought to be done? "I do most certainly." Adapt your præcognitions then to the present matter. Here the dispute begins. Agamemnon says, "I ought not to give up Chryseis to her father." Achilles says, "You ought." It is certain that one of the two makes a wrong adaptation of the præcognition of "ought" or "duty." Further, Agamemnon says, "Then if I ought to restore Chryseis, it is fit that I take his prize from some of you." Achilles replies, "Would you then take her whom I love?" "Yes, her whom you love." "Must I then be the only man who goes without a prize? and must I be the only man who has no prize?" Thus the dispute begins.

What then is education? Education is the learning how to adapt the natural præcognitions to the particular things conformably to nature; and then to distinguish that of things some are in our power, but others are not. In our power are will and all acts which depend on the will; things not in our power are the body, the parts of the body, possessions, parents, brothers, children, country, and, generally, all with whom we live in society. In what then should we place the good? To what kind of things ([Greek: ousia]) shall we adapt it? To the things which are in our power? Is not health then a good thing, and soundness of limb, and life, and are not children and parents and country? Who will tolerate you if you deny this?

Let us then transfer the notion of good to these things. Is it possible, then, when a man sustains damage and does not obtain good things, that he can be happy? It is not possible. And can he maintain towards society a proper behavior? He can not. For I am naturally formed to look after my own interest. If it is my interest to have an estate in land, it is my interest also to take it from my neighbor. If it is my interest to have a garment, it is my interest also to steal it from the bath. This is the origin of wars, civil commotions, tyrannies, conspiracies. And how shall I be still able to maintain my duty towards Zeus? For if I sustain damage and am unlucky, he takes no care of me. And what is he to me if he cannot help me? And further, what is he to me if he allows me to be in the condition in which I am? I now begin to hate him. Why then do we build temples, why setup statues to Zeus, as well as to evil demons, such as to Fever; and how is Zeus the Saviour, and how the giver of rain, and the giver of fruits? And in truth if we place the nature of Good in any such things, all this follows.

What should we do then? This is the inquiry of the true philosopher who is in labor. Now I do not see what the good is nor the bad. Am I not mad? Yes. But suppose that I place the good somewhere among the things which depend on the will; all will laugh at me. There will come some greyhead wearing many gold rings on his fingers, and he will shake his head and say: "Hear, my child. It is right that you should philosophize; but you ought to have some brains also; all this that you are doing is silly. You learn the syllogism from philosophers; but you know how to act better than philosophers do." Man why then do you blame me, if I know? What shall I say to this slave? If I am silent, he will burst. I must speak in this way: "Excuse me, as you would excuse lovers; I am not my own master; I am mad."

HOW WE SHOULD STRUGGLE WITH CIRCUMSTANCES.—
It is circumstances (difficulties) which show what men are. Therefore when a difficulty falls upon you, remember that God, like a trainer of wrestlers, has matched you with a rough young

man. For what purpose? you may say. Why, that you may become an Olympic conqueror; but it is not accomplished without sweat. In my opinion no man has had a more profitable difficulty than you have had, if you choose to make use of it as an athlete would deal with a young antagonist. We are now sending a scout to Rome; but no man sends a cowardly scout, who, if he only hears a noise and sees a shadow anywhere, comes running back in terror and reports that the enemy is close at hand. So now if you should come and tell us: "Fearful is the state of affairs at Rome; terrible is death; terrible is exile; terrible is calumny; terrible is poverty; fly, my friends, the enemy is near," we shall answer: "Begone, prophesy for yourself; we have committed only one fault, that we sent such a scout."

Diogenes, who was sent as a scout before you, made a different report to us. He says that death is no evil, for neither is it base; he says that fame (reputation) is the noise of madmen. And what has this spy said about pain, about pleasure, and about poverty? He says that to be naked is better than any purple robe, and to sleep on the bare ground is the softest bed; and he gives as a proof of each thing that he affirms his own courage, his tranquillity, his freedom, and the healthy appearance and compactness of his body. There is no enemy near, he says; all is peace. How so, Diogenes? "See," he replies, "if I am struck, if I have been wounded, if I have fled from any man." This is what a scout ought to be. But you come to us and tell us one thing after another. Will you not go back, and you will see clearer when you have laid aside fear?

ON THE SAME.—If these things are true, and if we are not silly, and are not acting hypocritically when we say that the good of man is in the will, and the evil too, and that everything else does not concern us, why are we still disturbed, why are we still afraid? The things about which we have been busied are in no man's power; and the things which are in the power of others, we care not for. What kind of trouble have we still?

But give me directions. Why should I give you directions? Has not Zeus given you directions? Has he not given to you what is your own free from hindrance and free from impediment, and what is not your own subject to hindrance and impediment? What directions then, what kind of orders did you bring when you came from him? Keep by every means what is your own; do not desire what belongs to others. Fidelity (integrity) is your own, virtuous shame is your own; who then can take these things from you? who else than yourself will hinder you from using them? But how do you act? When you seek what is not your own, you lose that which is your own. Having such promptings and commands from Zeus, what kind do you still ask from me? Am I more powerful than he, am I more worthy of confidence? But if you observe these, do you want any others besides? "Well, but he has not given these orders," you will say. Produce your præcognitions ([Greek: prolaepseis]), produce these proofs of philosophers, produce what you have often heard, and produce what you have said yourself, produce what you have read, produce what you have meditated on; and you will then see that all these things are from God.

If I have set my admiration on the poor body, I have given myself up to be a slave; if on my poor possessions, I also make myself a slave. For I immediately make it plain with what I may be caught; as if the snake draws in his head, I tell you to strike that part of him which he guards; and do you be assured that whatever part you choose to guard, that part your master will attack. Remembering this, whom will you still flatter or fear?

But I should like to sit where the Senators sit. Do you see that you are putting yourself in straits, you are squeezing yourself? How then shall I see well in any other way in the amphitheatre? Man, do not be a spectator at all, and you will not be squeezed. Why do you give yourself trouble? Or wait a little, and when the spectacle is over, seat yourself in the place reserved for the Senators and sun yourself. For remember this general truth, that it is we who squeeze ourselves, who put ourselves in straits; that is, our opinions squeeze us and put us in straits. For what is it to be reviled? Stand by a stone and revile it, and what will you gain? If then a man listens like a stone, what profit is there to the reviler? But if the reviler has as a stepping-stone (or ladder) the weakness of him who is reviled, then he accomplishes something. Strip him. What do you mean by him? Lay hold of his garment, strip it off. I have insulted you. Much good may it do you.

This was the practice of Socrates; this was the reason why he always had one face. But we choose to practise and study anything rather than the means by which we shall be unimpeded and free. You say: "Philosophers talk paradoxes." But are there no paradoxes in the other arts? And what is more paradoxical than to puncture a man's eye in order that he may see? If any one said this to a man ignorant of the surgical art, would he not ridicule the speaker? Where is the wonder, then, if in philosophy also many things which are true appear paradoxical to the inexperienced?

IN HOW MANY WAYS APPEARANCES EXIST, AND WHAT AIDS WE SHOULD PROVIDE AGAINST THEM.—Appearances are to us in four ways. For either things appear as they are; or they are not, and do not even appear to be; or they are, and do not appear to be; or they are not, and yet appear to be. Further, in all these cases to form a right judgment (to hit the mark) is the office of an educated man. But whatever it is that annoys (troubles) us, to that we ought to apply a remedy. If the sophisms of Pyrrho and of the Academics are what annoys (troubles), we must apply the remedy to them. If it is the persuasion of appearances, by which some things appear to be good, when they are not good, let us seek a remedy for this. If it is habit which annoys us, we must try to seek aid against habit. What aid, then, can we find against habit? The contrary habit. You hear the ignorant say: "That unfortunate person is dead; his father and mother are overpowered with sorrow; he was cut off by an untimely death and in a foreign land." Hear the contrary way of speaking. Tear yourself from these expressions; oppose to one habit the contrary habit; to sophistry oppose reason, and the exercise and discipline of reason; against persuasive (deceitful) appearances we ought to have manifest præcognitions ([Greek: prolaepseis]), cleared of all impurities and ready to hand.

When death appears an evil, we ought to have this rule in readiness, that it is fit to avoid evil things, and that death is a necessary thing. For what shall I do, and where shall I escape it? Suppose that I am not Sarpedon, the son of Zeus, nor able to speak in this noble way. I will go and I am resolved either to behave bravely myself or to give to another the opportunity of doing so; if I cannot succeed in doing anything myself, I will not grudge another the doing of something noble. Suppose that it is above our power to act thus; is it not in our power to reason thus? Tell me where I can escape death; discover for me the country, show me the men to whom I must go, whom death does not visit. Discover to me a charm against death. If I have not one, what do you wish me to do? I cannot escape from death. Shall I not escape from the fear of death, but shall I die lamenting and trembling? For the origin of perturbation is this, to wish for something, and that this should not happen. Therefore if I am able to change externals according to my wish, I change them; but if I cannot, I am ready to tear out the eyes of him who hinders me. For the nature of man is not to endure to be deprived of the good, and not to endure the falling into the evil. Then at last, when I am neither able to change circumstances nor to tear out the eyes of him who hinders me, I sit down and groan, and abuse whom I can, Zeus and the rest of the gods. For if they do not care for me, what are they to me? Yes, but you will be an impious man. In what respect, then, will it be worse for me than it is now? To sum up, remember that unless piety and your interest be in the same thing, piety cannot be maintained in any man. Do not these things seem necessary (true)?

THAT WE OUGHT NOT TO BE ANGRY WITH MEN; AND WHAT ARE THE SMALL AND THE GREAT THINGS AMONG MEN.—What is the cause of assenting to anything? The fact that it appears to be true. It is not possible then to assent to that which appears not to be true. Why? Because this is the nature of the understanding, to incline to the true, to be dissatisfied with the false, and in matters uncertain to withhold assent. What is the proof of this? Imagine (persuade yourself), if you can, that it is now night. It is not possible. Take away your persuasion that it is day. It is not possible. Persuade yourself or take away your persuasion that the stars are even in number. It is impossible. When then any man assents to that which is false, be assured that he did not intend to assent to it as false, for every soul is unwillingly deprived of the truth, as Plato says; but the falsity seemed to him to be true. Well, in acts what have we of the like kind as we have here truth or falsehood? We have the fit and the not fit (duty and not duty), the profitable and the unprofitable, that which is suitable to a person and that which is not, and whatever is like these. Can then a man think that a thing is useful to him and not choose it? He cannot. How says Medea?

"'Tis true I know what evil I shall do,
But passion overpowers the better counsel."

She thought that to indulge her passion and take vengeance on her husband was more profitable than to spare her children. It was so; but she was deceived. Show her plainly that she is deceived, and she will not do it; but so long as you do not show it, what can she follow except that which appears to herself (her opinion)? Nothing else. Why then are you angry with the unhappy woman that she has been bewildered about the most important things, and is become a viper instead of a human creature? And why not, if it is possible, rather pity, as we pity the blind and the lame, so those who are blinded and maimed in the faculties which are supreme?

Whoever then clearly remembers this, that to man the measure of every act is the appearance (the opinion), whether the thing appears good or bad. If good, he is free from blame; if bad, himself suffers the penalty, for it is impossible that he who is deceived can be one person, and he who suffers another person—whoever remembers this will not be angry with any man, will not be vexed at any man, will not revile or blame any man, nor hate, nor quarrel with any man.

So then all these great and dreadful deeds have this origin, in the appearance (opinion)? Yes, this origin and no other. The Iliad is nothing else than appearance and the use of appearances. It appeared to Alexander to carry off the wife of Menelaus. It appeared to Helene to follow him. If then it had appeared to Menelaus to feel that it was a gain to be deprived of such a wife, what would have happened? Not only would the Iliad have been lost, but the Odyssey also. On so small a matter then did such great things depend? But what do you mean by such great things? Wars and civil commotions, and the destruction of many men and cities. And what great matter is this? Is it nothing? But what great matter is the death of many oxen, and many sheep, and many nests of swallows or storks being burnt or destroyed? Are these things then like those? Very like. Bodies of men are destroyed, and the bodies of oxen and sheep; the dwellings of men are burnt, and the nests of storks. What is there in this great or dreadful? Or show me what is the difference between a man's house and a stork's nest, as far as each is a dwelling; except that man builds his little houses of beams and tiles and bricks, and the stork builds them of sticks and mud. Are a stork and a man then like things? What say you? In body they are very much alike.

Does a man then differ in no respect from a stork? Don't suppose that I say so; but there is no difference in these matters (which I have mentioned). In what then is the difference? Seek and you will find that there is a difference in another matter. See whether it is not in a man the understanding of what he does, see if it is not in social community, in fidelity, in modesty, in steadfastness, in intelligence. Where then is the great good and evil in men? It is where the difference is. If the difference is preserved and remains fenced round, and neither modesty is destroyed, nor fidelity, nor intelligence, then the man also is preserved; but if any of these things is destroyed and stormed like a city, then the man too perishes: and in this consist the great things. Alexander, you say, sustained great damage then when the Hellenes invaded and when they ravaged Troy, and when his brothers perished. By no means; for no man is damaged by an action which is not his own; but what happened at that time was only the destruction of stork's nests. Now the ruin of Alexander was when he lost the character of modesty, fidelity, regard to hospitality, and to decency. When was Achilles ruined? Was it when Patroclus died? Not so. But it happened when he began to be angry, when he wept for a girl, when he forgot that he was at Troy not to get mistresses, but to fight. These things are the ruin of men, this is being besieged, this is the destruction of cities, when right opinions are destroyed, when they are corrupted.

ON CONSTANCY (OR FIRMNESS).—The being (nature) of

the good is a certain will; the being of the bad is a certain kind of will. What, then, are externals? Materials for the will, about which the will being conversant shall obtain its own good or evil. How shall it obtain the good? If it does not admire (overvalue) the materials; for the opinions about the materials, if the opinions are right, make the will good: but perverse and distorted opinions make the will bad. God has fixed this law, and says, "If you would have anything good, receive it from yourself." You say, No, but I will have it from another. Do not so: but receive it from yourself. Therefore when the tyrant threatens and calls me, I say, Whom do you threaten? If he says, I will put you in chains, I say, You threaten my hands and my feet. If he says, I will cut off your head, I reply, You threaten my head. If he says, I will throw you into prison, I say, You threaten the whole of this poor body. If he threatens me with banishment, I say the same. Does he then not threaten you at all? If I feel that all these things do not concern me, he does not threaten me at all; but if I fear any of them, it is I whom he threatens. Whom then do I fear? the master of what? The master of things which are in my own power? There is no such master. Do I fear the master of things which are not in my power? And what are these things to me?

Do you philosophers then teach us to despise kings? I hope not. Who among us teaches to claim against them the power over things which they possess? Take my poor body, take my property, take my reputation, take those who are about me. If I advise any persons to claim these things, they may truly accuse me. Yes, but I intend to command your opinions also. And who has given you this power? How can you conquer the opinion of another man? By applying terror to it, he replies, I will conquer it. Do you not know that opinion conquers itself, and is not conquered by another? But nothing else can conquer will except the will itself. For this reason too the law of God is most powerful and most just, which is this: Let the stronger always be superior to the weaker. Ten are stronger than one. For what? For putting in chains, for killing, for dragging whither they choose, for taking away what a man has. The ten therefore conquer the one in this in which they are stronger. In what then are the ten weaker? If the one possesses right opinions and the others do not. Well then, can the ten conquer in this matter? How is it possible? If we were placed in the scales, must not the heavier draw down the scale in which it is.

How strange then that Socrates should have been so treated by the Athenians. Slave, why do you say Socrates? Speak of the thing as it is: how strange that the poor body of Socrates should have been carried off and dragged to prison by stronger men, and that anyone should have given hemlock to the poor body of Socrates, and that it should breathe out the life. Do these things seem strange, do they seem unjust, do you on account of these things blame God? Had Socrates then no equivalent for these things? Where then for him was the nature of good? Whom shall we listen to, you or him? And what does Socrates say? "Anytus and Melitus can kill me, but they cannot hurt me." And further, he says, "If it so pleases God, so let it be."

But show me that he who has the inferior principles overpowers him who is superior in principles. You will never show this, nor come near showing it; for this is the law of nature and of God that the superior shall always overpower the inferior. In what? In that in which it is superior. One body is stronger than another: many are stronger than one: the thief is stronger than he who is not a thief. This is the reason why I also lost my lamp, because in wakefulness the thief was superior to me. But the man bought the lamp at this price: for a lamp he became a thief, a faithless fellow, and like a wild beast. This seemed to him a good bargain. Be it so. But a man has seized me by the cloak, and is drawing me to the public place: then others bawl out, Philosopher, what has been the use of your opinions? see, you are dragged to prison, you are going to be beheaded. And what system of philosophy ([Greek: eisagogaen)] could I have made so that, if a stronger man should have laid hold of my cloak, I should not be dragged off; that if ten men should have laid hold of me and cast me into prison, I should not be cast in? Have I learned nothing else then? I have learned to see that everything which happens, if it be independent of my will, is nothing to me. I may ask, if you have not gained by this. Why then do you seek advantage in anything else than in that in which you have learned that advantage is?

Will you not leave the small arguments ([Greek: logaria]) about these matters to others, to lazy fellows, that they may sit in a corner and receive their sorry pay, or grumble that no one gives them anything; and will you not come forward and make use of what you have learned? For it is not these small arguments that are wanted now; the writings of the Stoics are full of them. What then is the thing which is wanted? A man who shall apply them, one who by his acts shall bear testimony to his words. Assume, I intreat you, this character, that we may no longer use in the schools the examples of the ancients, but may have some example of our own.

To whom then does the contemplation of these matters (philosophical inquiries) belong? To him who has leisure, for man is an animal that loves contemplation. But it is shameful to contemplate these things as runaway slaves do; we should sit, as in a theatre, free from distraction, and listen at one time to the tragic actor, at another time to the lute-player; and not do as slaves do. As soon as the slave has taken his station he praises the actor and at the same time looks round; then if any one calls out his master's name, the slave is immediately frightened and disturbed. It is shameful for philosophers thus to contemplate the works of nature. For what is a master? Man is not the master of man; but death is, and life and pleasure and pain; for if he comes without these things, bring Cæsar to me and you will see how firm I am. But when he shall come with these things, thundering and lightning, and when I am afraid of them, what do I do then except to recognize my master like the runaway slave? But so long as I have any respite from these terrors, as a runaway slave stands in the theatre, so do I. I bathe, I drink, I sing; but all this I do with terror and uneasiness. But if I shall release myself from my masters, that is from those things by means of which masters are formidable, what further trouble have I, what master have I still?

What then, ought we to publish these things to all men? No, but we ought to accommodate ourselves to the ignorant ([Greek: tois idiotais]) and to say: "This man recommends to me that which he thinks good for himself. I excuse him." For Socrates also excused the jailer who had the charge of him in prison and was weeping when Socrates was going to drink the poison, and said, "How generously he laments over us." Does he then say to the jailer that for this reason we have sent away the women? No, but he says it to his friends who were able to hear (understand) it; and he treats the jailer as a child.

THAT CONFIDENCE (COURAGE) IS NOT INCONSISTENT WITH CAUTION.—The opinion of the philosophers perhaps seem to some to be a paradox; but still let us examine as well as we can, if it is true that it is possible to do everything both with caution and with confidence. For caution seems to be in a manner contrary to confidence, and contraries are in no way consistent. That which seems to many to be a paradox in the matter under consideration in my opinion is of this kind; if we asserted that we ought to employ caution and confidence in the same things, men might justly accuse us of bringing together things which cannot be united. But now where is the difficulty in what is said? for if these things are true, which have been often said and often proved, that the nature of good is in the use of appearances, and the nature of evil likewise, and that things independent of our will do not admit either the nature of evil or of good, what paradox do the philosophers assert if they say that where things are not dependent on the will, there you should employ confidence, but where they are dependent on the will, there you should employ caution? For if the bad consists in the bad exercise of the will, caution ought only to be used where things are dependent on the will. But if things independent of the will and not in our power are nothing to us, with respect to these we must employ confidence; and thus we shall both be cautious and confident, and indeed confident because of our caution. For by employing caution towards things which are really bad, it will result that we shall have confidence with respect to things which are not so.

We are then in the condition of deer; when they flee from the huntsmen's feathers in fright, whither do they turn and in what do they seek refuge as safe? They turn to the nets, and thus they perish by confounding things which are objects of fear with things that they ought not to fear. Thus we also act: in what cases do we fear? In things which are independent of the will. In what cases on the contrary do we behave with confidence, as if there were no danger? In things dependent on the will. To be deceived then, or to act rashly, or shamelessly, or with base desire to seek something, does not concern us at all, if we only hit the mark in things which are independent of our will. But where there is death or exile or pain or infamy, there we attempt to run away, there we are struck with terror. Therefore, as we may expect it to happen with those who err in the greatest matters, we convert natural confidence (that is, according to nature) into audacity, desperation, rashness, shamelessness; and we convert natural caution and modesty into cowardice and meanness, which are full of fear and confusion. For if a man should transfer caution to those things in which the will may be exercised and the acts of the will, he will immediately by willing to be cautious have also the power of avoiding what he chooses; but if he transfer it to the things which are not in his power and will, and attempt to avoid the things which are in the power of others, he will of necessity fear, he will be unstable, he will be disturbed; for death or pain is not formidable, but the fear of pain or death. For this reason we commend the poet, who said:

"Not death is evil, but a shameful death."

Confidence (courage) then ought to be employed against death, and caution against the fear of death. But now we do the contrary, and employ against death the attempt to escape; and to our opinion about it we employ carelessness, rashness, and indifference. These things Socrates properly used to call tragic masks; for as to children masks appear terrible and fearful from inexperience, we also are affected in like manner by events (the things which happen in life) for no other reason than children are by masks. For what is a child? Ignorance. What is a child? Want of knowledge. For when a child knows these things, he is in no way inferior to us. What is death? A tragic mask. Turn it and examine it. See, it does not bite. The poor body must be separated from the spirit either now or later as it was separated from it before. Why then are you troubled if it be separated now? for if it is not separated now, it will be separated afterwards. Why? That the period of the universe may be completed, for it has need of the present, and of the future, and of the past. What is pain? A mask. Turn it and examine it. The poor flesh is moved roughly, then on the contrary smoothly. If this does not satisfy (please) you, the door is open; if it does, bear (with things). For the door ought to be open for all occasions; and so we have no trouble.

What then is the fruit of these opinions? It is that which ought to be the most noble and the most becoming to those who are really educated, release from perturbation, release from fear. Freedom. For in these matters we must not believe the many, who say that free persons only ought to be educated, but we should rather believe the philosophers who say that the educated only are free. How is this? In this manner: Is freedom anything else than the power of living as we choose? Nothing else. Tell me then, ye men, do you wish to live in error? We do not. No one then who lives in error is free. Do you wish to live in fear? Do you wish to live in sorrow? Do you wish to live in perturbation? By no means. No one then who is in a state of fear or sorrow or perturbation is free; but whoever is delivered from sorrows and fears and perturbations, he is at the same time also delivered from servitude. How then can we continue to believe you, most dear legislators, when you say, We only allow free persons to be educated? For philosophers say we allow none to be free except the educated; that is, God does not allow it. When then a man has turned round before the prætor his own slave, has he done nothing? He has done something. What? He has turned round his own slave before the prætor. Has he done nothing more? Yes: he is also bound to pay for him the tax called the twentieth. Well then, is not the man who has gone through this ceremony become free? No more than he is become free from perturbations. Have you who are able to turn round (free) others no master? is not money your master, or a girl or a boy, or some tyrant or some friend of the tyrant? Why do you trouble then when you are going off to any trial (danger) of this kind? It is for this reason that I often say, study and hold in readiness these principles by which you may determine what those things are with reference to which you ought to be cautious, courageous in that which does not depend on your will, cautious in that which does depend on it.

OF TRANQUILLITY (FREEDOM FROM PERTURBATION).—Consider, you who are going into court, what you wish to maintain and what you wish to succeed in. For if you wish to maintain a will conformable to nature, you have every security, every facility, you have no troubles. For if you wish to maintain what is in your own power and is naturally free, and if you are content with these, what else do you care for? For who is the master of such things? Who can take them away? If you choose to be modest and faithful, who shall not allow you to be so? If you choose not to be restrained or compelled, who shall compel you to desire what you think that you ought not to desire? who shall compel you to avoid what you do not think fit to avoid? But what do you say? The judge will determine against you something that appears formidable; but that you should also suffer in trying to avoid it, how can he do that? When then the pursuit of objects and the avoiding of them are in your power, what else do you care for? Let this be your preface, this your narrative, this your confirmation, this your victory, this your peroration, this your applause (or the approbation which you will receive).

Therefore Socrates said to one who was reminding him to prepare for his trial, Do you not think then that I have been preparing for it all my life? By what kind of preparation? I have maintained that which was in my own power. How then? I have never done anything unjust either in my private or in my public life.

But if you wish to maintain externals also, your poor body, your little property, and your little estimation, I advise you to make from this moment all possible preparation, and then consider both the nature of your judge and your adversary. If it is necessary to embrace his knees, embrace his knees; if to weep, weep; if to groan, groan. For when you have subjected to externals what is your own, then be a slave and do not resist, and do not sometimes choose to be a slave, and sometimes not choose, but with all your mind be one or the other, either free or a slave, either instructed or uninstructed, either a well-bred cock or a mean one, either endure to be beaten until you die or yield at once; and let it not happen to you to receive many stripes and then to yield. But if these things are base, determine immediately. Where is the nature of evil and good? It is where truth is: where truth is and where nature is, there is caution: where truth is, there is courage where nature is.

For this reason also it is ridiculous to say, Suggest something to me (tell me what to do). What should I suggest to you? Well, form my mind so as to accommodate itself to any event. Why that is just the same as if a man who is ignorant of letters should say, Tell me what to write when any name is proposed to me. For if I should tell him to write Dion, and then another should come and propose to him not the name of Dion but that of Theon, what will be done? what will he write? But if you have practised writing, you are also prepared to write (or to do) anything that is required. If you are not, what can I now suggest? For if circumstances require something else, what will you say, or what will you do? Remember then this general precept and you will need no suggestion. But if you gape after externals, you must of necessity ramble up and down in obedience to the will of your master. And who is the master? He who has the power over the things which you seek to gain or try to avoid.

HOW MAGNANIMITY IS CONSISTENT WITH CARE.— Things themselves (materials) are indifferent; but the use of them is not indifferent. How then shall a man preserve firmness and tranquillity, and at the same time be careful and neither rash nor negligent? If he imitates those who play at dice. The counters are indifferent; the dice are indifferent. How do I know what the cast will be? But to use carefully and dexterously the cast of the dice, this is my business. Thus then in life also the chief business is this: distinguish and separate things, and say: Externals are not in my power: will is in my power. Where shall I seek the good and the bad? Within, in the things which are my own. But in what does not belong to you call nothing either good or bad, or profit or damage or anything of the kind.

What then? Should we use such things carelessly? In no way: for this on the other hand is bad for the faculty of the will, and consequently against nature; but we should act carefully because the use is not indifferent, and we should also act with firmness and freedom from perturbations because the material is indifferent. For where the material is not indifferent, there no man can hinder me or compel me. Where I can be hindered and compelled, the obtaining of those things is not in my power, nor is it good or bad; but the use is either bad or good, and the use is in my power. But it is difficult to mingle and to bring together these two things—the carefulness of him who is affected by the matter (or things about him), and the firmness of him who has no regard for it; but it is not impossible: and if it is, happiness is impossible. But we should act as we do in the case of a voyage. What can I do? I can choose the master of the ship, the sailors, the day, the opportunity. Then comes a storm. What more have I to care for? for my part is done. The business belongs to another, the master. But the ship is sinking—what then have I to do? I do the only thing that I can, not to be drowned full of fear, nor screaming nor blaming God, but knowing that what has been produced must also perish: for I am not an immortal being, but a man, a part of the whole, as an hour is a part of the day: I must be present like the hour, and past like the hour. What difference then does it make to me how I pass away, whether by being suffocated or by a fever, for I must pass through some such means.

How then is it said that some external things are according to nature and others contrary to nature? It is said as it might be said if we were separated from union (or society): for to the foot I shall say that it is according to nature for it to be clean; but if you take it as a foot and as a thing not detached (independent), it will befit it both to step into the mud and tread on thorns, and sometimes to be cut off for the good of the whole body; otherwise it is no longer a foot. We should think in some such way about ourselves also. What are you? A man. If you consider yourself as detached from other men, it is according to nature to live to old age, to be rich, to be healthy. But if you consider yourself as a man and a part of a certain whole, it is for the sake of that whole that at one time you should be sick, at another time take a voyage and run into danger, and at another time be in want, and in some cases die prematurely. Why then are you troubled? Do you not know, that as a foot is no longer a foot if it is detached from the body, so you are no longer a man if you are separated from other men. For what is a man? A part of a state, of that first which consists of gods and of men; then of that which is called next to it, which is a small image of the universal state. What then must I be brought to trial; must another have a fever, another sail on the sea, another die, and another be condemned? Yes, for it is impossible in such a universe of things, among so many living together, that such things should not happen, some to one and others to others. It is your duty then since you are come here, to say what you ought, to arrange these things as it is fit. Then some one says, "I shall charge you with doing me wrong." Much good may it do you: I have done my part; but whether you also have done yours, you must look to that; for there is some danger of this too, that it may escape your notice.

OF INDIFFERENCE.—The hypothetical proposition is indifferent: the judgment about it is not indifferent, but it is either knowledge or opinion or error. Thus life is indifferent: the use is not indifferent. When any man then tells you that these things also are indifferent, do not become negligent; and when a man invites you to be careful (about such things), do not become abject and struck with admiration of material things. And it is good for you to know your own preparation and power, that in those matters where you have not been prepared, you may keep quiet, and not be vexed, if others have the advantage over you. For you too in syllogisms will claim to have the advantage over them; and if others should be vexed at this, you will console them by saying, "I have learned them, and you have not." Thus also where there is need of any practice, seek not that which is acquired from the need (of such practice), but yield in that matter to those who have had practice, and be yourself content with firmness of mind.

Go and salute a certain person. How? Not meanly. But I have been shut out, for I have not learned to make my way through the window; and when I have found the door shut, I must either come back or enter through the window. But still speak to him. In what way? Not meanly. But suppose that you have not got what you wanted. Was this your business, and not his? Why then do you claim that which belongs to another? Always remember what is your own, and what belongs to another; and you will not be disturbed. Chrysippus therefore said well, So long as future things are uncertain, I always cling to those which are more adapted to the conservation of that which is according to nature; for God himself has given me the faculty of such choice. But if I knew that it was fated (in the order of things) for me to be sick, I would even move towards it; for the foot also, if it had intelligence, would move to go into the mud. For why are ears of corn produced? Is it not that they may become dry? And do they not become dry that they may be reaped? for they are not separated from communion with other things. If then they had perception, ought they to wish never to be reaped? But this is a curse upon ears of corn to be never reaped. So we must know that in the case of men too it is a curse not to die, just the same as not to be ripened and not to be reaped. But since we must be reaped, and we also know that we are reaped, we are vexed at it; for we neither know what we are nor have we studied what belongs to man, as those who have studied horses know what belongs to horses. But Chrysantas when he was going to strike the enemy checked himself when he heard the trumpet sounding a retreat: so it seemed better to him to obey the general's command than to follow his own inclination. But not one of us chooses, even when necessity summons, readily to obey it, but weeping and groaning we suffer what we do suffer, and we call them "circumstances." What kind of circumstances, man? If you give the name of circumstances to the things which are around you, all things are circumstances; but if you call hardships by this name, what hardship is there in the dying of that which has been produced? But that which destroys is either a sword, or a wheel, or the sea, or a tile, or a tyrant. Why do you care about the way of going down to Hades? All ways are equal. But if you will listen to the truth, the way which the tyrant sends you is shorter. A tyrant never killed a man in six months: but a fever is often a year about it. All these things are only sound and the noise of empty names.

HOW WE OUGHT TO USE DIVINATION.—Through an unreasonable regard to divination many of us omit many duties. For what more can the diviner see than death or danger or disease, or generally things of that kind? If then I must expose myself to danger for a friend, and if it is my duty even to die for him, what need have I then for divination? Have I not within me a diviner who has told me the nature of good and of evil, and has explained to me the signs (or marks) of both? What need have I then to consult the viscera of victims or the flight of birds, and why do I submit when he says, It is for your interest? For does he know what is for my interest, does he know what is good; and as he has learned the signs of the viscera, has he also learned the signs of good and evil? For if he knows the signs of these, he knows the signs both of the beautiful and of the ugly, and of the just and of the unjust. Do you tell me, man, what is the thing which is signified for me: is it life or death, poverty or wealth? But whether these things are for my interest or whether they are not, I do not intend to ask you. Why don't you give your opinion on matters of grammar, and why do you give it here about things on which we are all in error and disputing with one another?

What then leads us to frequent use of divination? Cowardice, the dread of what will happen. This is the reason why we flatter the diviners. Pray, master, shall I succeed to the property of my father? Let us see: let us sacrifice on the occasion. Yes, master, as fortune chooses. When he has said, You shall succeed to the inheritance, we thank him as if we received the inheritance from him. The consequence is that they play upon us.

Will you not then seek the nature of good in the rational animal? for if it is not there, you will not choose to say that it exists in any other thing (plant or animal). What then? are not plants and animals also the works of God? They are; but they are not superior things, nor yet parts of the gods. But you are a superior thing; you are a portion separated from the Deity; you have in yourself a certain portion of him. Why then are you ignorant of your own noble descent? Why do you not know whence you came? will you not remember when you are eating who you are who eat and whom you feed? When you are in social intercourse, when you are exercising yourself, when you are engaged in discussion, know you not that you are nourishing a god, that you are exercising a god? Wretch, you are carrying about a god with you, and you know it not. Do you think that I mean some god of silver or of gold, and external? You carry him within yourself, and you perceive not that you are polluting him by impure thoughts and dirty deeds. And if an image of God were present, you would not dare to do any of the things which you are doing; but when God himself is present within and sees all and hears all, you are not ashamed of thinking such things and doing such things, ignorant as you are of your own nature and subject to the anger of God. Then why do we fear when we are sending a young man from the school into active life, lest he should do anything improperly, eat improperly, have improper intercourse with women; and lest the rags in which he is wrapped should debase him, lest fine garments should make him proud. This youth (if he acts thus) does not know his own God; he knows not with whom he sets out (into the world). But can we endure when he says, "I wish I had you (God) with me." Have you not God with you? and do you seek for any other when you have him? or will God tell you anything else than this? If you were a statue of Phidias, either Athena or Zeus, you would think both of yourself and of the artist, and if you had any understanding (power of perception) you would try to do nothing unworthy of him who made you or of yourself, and try not to appear in an unbecoming dress (attitude) to those who look upon you. But now because Zeus has made you, for this reason do you care not how you shall appear? And yet is the artist (in the one case) like the artist in the other? or the work in the one case like the other? And what work of an artist, for instance, has in itself the faculties, which the artist shows in making it? Is it not marble or bronze, or gold or ivory? and the Athena of Phidias, when she has once extended the hand and received in it the figure of Victory, stands in that attitude for ever. But the works of God have power of motion, they breathe, they have the faculty of using the appearances of things and the power of examining them. Being the work of such an artist do you dishonor him? And what shall I say, not only that he made you, but also entrusted you to yourself and made you a deposit to yourself? Will you not think of this too, but do you also dishonor your guardianship? But if God had entrusted an orphan to you, would you thus neglect him? He has delivered yourself to your own care, and says: "I had no one fitter to entrust him to than yourself; keep him for me such as he is by nature, modest, faithful, erect, unterrified, free from passion and perturbation." And then you do not keep him such.

But some will say, Whence has this fellow got the arrogance

which he displays and these supercilious looks? I have not yet so much gravity as befits a philosopher; for I do not yet feel confidence in what I have learned and in what I have assented to. I still fear my own weakness. Let me get confidence and then you shall see a countenance such as I ought to have and an attitude such as I ought to have; then I will show to you the statue, when it is perfected, when it is polished. What do you expect? a supercilious countenance? Does the Zeus at Olympia lift up his brow? No, his look is fixed as becomes him who is ready to say:

Irrevocable is my word and shall not fail.—Iliad, i., 526.

Such will I show myself to you, faithful, modest, noble, free from perturbation. What, and immortal, too, except from old age, and from sickness? No, but dying as becomes a god, sickening as becomes a god. This power I possess; this I can do. But the rest I do not possess, nor can I do. I will show the nerves (strength) of a philosopher. What nerves are these? A desire never disappointed, an aversion which never falls on that which it would avoid, a proper pursuit ([Greek: hormaen]), a diligent purpose, an assent which is not rash. These you shall see.

THAT WHEN WE CANNOT FULFIL THAT WHICH THE CHARACTER OF A MAN PROMISES, WE ASSUME THE CHARACTER OF A PHILOSOPHER.—It is no common (easy) thing to do this only, to fulfil the promise of a man's nature. For what is a man? The answer is, A rational and mortal being. Then by the rational faculty from whom are we separated? From wild beasts. And from what others? From sheep and like animals. Take care then to do nothing like a wild beast; but if you do, you have lost the character of a man; you have not fulfilled your promise. See that you do nothing like a sheep; but if you do, in this case also the man is lost. What then do we do as sheep? When we act gluttonously, when we act lewdly, when we act rashly, filthily, inconsiderately, to what have we declined? To sheep. What have we lost? The rational faculty. When we act contentiously and harmfully and passionately and violently, to what have we declined? To wild beasts. Consequently some of us are great wild beasts, and others little beasts, of a bad disposition and small, whence we may say, Let me be eaten by a lion. But in all these ways the promise of a man acting as a man is destroyed. For when is a conjunctive (complex) proposition maintained? When it fulfils what its nature promises; so that the preservation of a complex proposition is when it is a conjunction of truths. When is a disjunctive maintained? When it fulfils what it promises. When are flutes, a lyre, a horse, a dog, preserved? (When they severally keep their promise.) What is the wonder then if man also in like manner is preserved, and in like manner is lost? Each man is improved and preserved by corresponding acts, the carpenter by acts of carpentry, the grammarian by acts of grammar. But if a man accustoms himself to write ungrammatically, of necessity his art will be corrupted and destroyed. Thus modest actions preserve the modest man, and immodest actions destroy him; and actions of fidelity preserve the faithful man, and the contrary actions destroy him. And on the other hand contrary actions strengthen contrary characters: shamelessness strengthens the shameless man, faithlessness the faithless man, abusive words the abusive man, anger the man of an angry temper, and unequal receiving and giving make the avaricious man more avaricious.

For this reason philosophers admonish us not to be satisfied with learning only, but also to add study, and then practice. For we have long been accustomed to do contrary things, and we put in practice opinions which are contrary to true opinions. If then we shall not also put in practice right opinions, we shall be nothing more than the expositors of the opinions of others. For now who among us is not able to discourse according to the rules of art about good and evil things (in this fashion)? That of things some are good, and some are bad, and some are indifferent: the good then are virtues, and the things which participate in virtues; and the bad are the contrary; and the indifferent are wealth, health, reputation. Then, if in the midst of our talk there should happen some greater noise than usual, or some of those who are present should laugh at us, we are disturbed. Philosopher, where are the things which you were talking about? Whence did you produce and utter them? From the lips, and thence only. Why then do you corrupt the aids provided by others? Why do you treat the weightiest matters as if you were playing a game of dice? For it is one thing to lay up bread and wine as in a storehouse, and another thing to eat. That which has been eaten, is digested, distributed, and is become sinews, flesh, bones, blood, healthy color, healthy breath. Whatever is stored up, when you choose you can readily take and show it; but you have no other advantage from it except so far as to appear to possess it. For what is the difference between explaining these doctrines and those of men who have different opinions? Sit down now and explain according to the rules of art the opinions of Epicurus, and perhaps you will explain his opinions in a more useful manner than Epicurus himself. Why then do you call yourself a Stoic? Why do you deceive the many? Why do you act the part of a Jew, when you are a Greek? Do you not see how (why) each is called a Jew, or a Syrian, or an Egyptian? and when we see a man inclining to two sides, we are accustomed to say, This man is not a Jew, but he acts as one. But when he has assumed the affects of one who has been imbued with Jewish doctrine and has adopted that sect, then he is in fact and he is named a Jew.

HOW WE MAY DISCOVER THE DUTIES OF LIFE FROM NAMES.—Consider who you are. In the first place, you are a man; and this is one who has nothing superior to the faculty of the will, but all other things subjected to it; and the faculty itself he possesses unenslaved and free from subjection. Consider then from what things you have been separated by reason. You have been separated from wild beasts; you have been separated from domestic animals ([Greek: probaton]). Further, you are a citizen of the world, and a part of it, not one of the subservient (serving), but one of the principal (ruling) parts, for you are capable of comprehending the divine administration and of considering the connection of things. What then does the character of a citizen promise (profess)? To hold nothing as profitable to himself; to deliberate about nothing as if he were detached from the community, but to act as the hand or foot would do, if they had reason and understood the constitution of nature, for they would never put themselves in motion nor desire anything otherwise than with reference to the whole. Therefore, the philosophers say well, that if the good man had foreknowledge of what would happen, he would co-operate towards his own sickness and death and mutilation, since he knows that these things are assigned to him according to the universal arrangement, and that the whole is superior to the part, and the state to the citizen. But now because we do not know the future, it is our duty to stick to the things which are in their nature more suitable for our choice, for we were made among other things for this.

After this, remember that you are a son. What does this character promise? To consider that everything which is the son's belongs to the father, to obey him in all things, never to blame him to another, nor to say or do anything which does him injury, to yield to him in all things and give way, co-operating with him as far as you can. After this know that you are a brother also, and that to this character it is due to make concessions; to be easily persuaded, to speak good of your brother, never to claim in opposition to him any of the things which are independent of the will, but readily to give them up, that you may have the larger share in what is dependent on the will. For see what a thing it is, in place of a lettuce, if it should so happen, or a seat, to gain for yourself goodness of disposition. How great is the advantage.

Next to this, if you are a senator of any state, remember that you are a senator; if a youth, that you are a youth; if an old man, that you are an old man; for each of such names, if it comes to be examined, marks out the proper duties. But if you go and blame your brother, I say to you, You have forgotten who you are and what is your name. In the next place, if you were a smith and made a wrong use of the hammer, you would have forgotten the smith; and if you have forgotten the brother and instead of a brother have become an enemy, would you appear not to have changed one thing for another in that case? And if instead of a man, who is a tame animal and social, you are become a mischievous wild beast, treacherous, and biting, have you lost nothing? But (I suppose) you must lose a bit of money that you may suffer damage? And does the loss of nothing else do a man damage? If you had lost the art of grammar or music, would you think the loss of it a damage? and if you shall lose modesty, moderation ([Greek: chtastolaen]) and gentleness, do you think the loss nothing? And yet the things first mentioned are lost by some cause external and independent of the will, and the second by our own fault; and as to the first neither to have them nor to lose them is shameful; but as to the second, not to have them and to lose them is shameful and matter of reproach and a misfortune.

What then? shall I not hurt him who has hurt me? In the first place consider what hurt ([Greek: blabae]) is, and remember what you have heard from the philosophers. For if the good consists in the will (purpose, intention, [Greek: proaireeis]), and the evil also in the will, see if what you say is not this: What then, since that man has hurt himself by doing an unjust act to me, shall I not hurt myself by doing some unjust act to him? Why do we not imagine to ourselves (mentally think of) something of this kind? But where there is any detriment to the body or to our possession, there is harm there; and where the same thing happens to the faculty of the will, there is (you suppose) no harm; for he who has been deceived or he who has done an unjust act neither suffers in the head nor in the eye nor in the hip, nor does he lose his estate; and we wish for nothing else than (security to) these things. But whether we shall have the will modest and faithful or shameless and faithless, we care not the least, except only in the school so far as a few words are concerned. Therefore our proficiency is limited to these few words; but beyond them it does not exist even in the slightest degree.

WHAT THE BEGINNING OF PHILOSOPHY IS.—The beginning of philosophy, to him at least who enters on it in the right way and by the door is a consciousness of his own weakness and inability about necessary things; for we come into the world with no natural notion of a right-angled triangle, or of a diesis (a quarter tone), or of a half-tone; but we learn each of these things by a certain transmission according to art; and for this reason those who do not know them do not think that they know them. But as to good and evil, and beautiful and ugly, and becoming and unbecoming, and happiness and misfortune, and proper and improper, and what we ought to do and what we ought not to do, who ever came into the world without having an innate idea of them? Wherefore we all use these names, and we endeavor to fit the preconceptions to the several cases (things) thus: he has done well; he has not done well; he has done as he ought, not as he ought; he has been unfortunate, he has been fortunate; he is unjust, he is just; who does not use these names? who among us defers the use of them till he has learned them, as he defers the use of the words about lines (geometrical figures) or sounds? And the cause of this is that we come into the world already taught as it were by nature some things on this matter ([Greek: topon]), and proceeding from these we have added to them self-conceit ([Greek: oiaesin]). For why, a man says, do I not know the beautiful and the ugly? Have I not the notion of it? You have. Do I not adapt it to particulars? You do. Do I not then adapt it properly? In that lies the whole question; and conceit is added here; for beginning from these things which are admitted men proceed to that which is matter of dispute by means of unsuitable adaptation; for if they possessed this power of adaptation in addition to those things, what would hinder them from being perfect? But now since you think that you properly adapt the preconceptions to the particulars, tell me whence you derive this (assume that you do so). Because I think so. But it does not seem so to another, and he thinks that he also makes a proper adaptation; or does he not think so? He does think so. Is it possible then that both of you can properly apply the preconceptions to things about which you have contrary opinions? It is not possible. Can you then show us anything better towards adapting the preconceptions beyond your thinking that you do? Does the madman do any other things than the things which seem to him right? Is then this criterion sufficient for him also? It is not sufficient. Come then to something which is superior to seeming ([Greek: tou dochein]). What is this?

Observe, this is the beginning of philosophy, a perception of the disagreement of men with one another, and an inquiry into the cause of the disagreement, and a condemnation and distrust of that which only "seems," and a certain investigation of that which "seems" whether it "seems" rightly, and a discovery of some rule ([Greek: chanonos]), as we have discovered a balance in the determination of weights, and a carpenter's rule (or square) in the case of straight and crooked things.—This is the beginning of philosophy. Must we say that all things are right which seem so to all? And how is it possible that contradictions can be right?—Not all then, but all which seem to us to be right.—How more to you than those which seem right to the

Syrians? why more than what seem right to the Egyptians? why more than what seems right to me or to any other man? Not at all more. What then "seems" to every man is not sufficient for determining what "is"; for neither in the case of weights nor measures are we satisfied with the bare appearance, but in each case we have discovered a certain rule. In this matter then is there no rule superior to what "seems"? And how is it possible that the most necessary things among men should have no sign (mark), and be incapable of being discovered? There is then some rule. And why then do we not seek the rule and discover it, and afterwards use it without varying from it, not even stretching out the finger without it? For this, I think, is that which when it is discovered cures of their madness those who use mere "seeming" as a measure, and misuse it; so that for the future proceeding from certain things (principles) known and made clear we may use in the case of particular things the preconceptions which are distinctly fixed.

What is the matter presented to us about which we are inquiring? Pleasure (for example). Subject it to the rule, throw it into the balance. Ought the good to be such a thing that it is fit that we have confidence in it? Yes. And in which we ought to confide? It ought to be. Is it fit to trust to anything which is insecure? No. Is then pleasure anything secure? No. Take it then and throw it out of the scale, and drive it far away from the place of good things. But if you are not sharp-sighted, and one balance is not enough for you, bring another. Is it fit to be elated over what is good? Yes. Is it proper then to be elated over present pleasure? See that you do not say that it is proper; but if you do, I shall then not think you worthy even of the balance. Thus things are tested and weighed when the rules are ready. And to philosophize is this, to examine and confirm the rules; and then to use them when they are known is the act of a wise and good man.

OF DISPUTATION OR DISCUSSION.—What things a man must learn in order to be able to apply the art of disputation, has been accurately shown by our philosophers (the Stoics); but with respect to the proper use of the things, we are entirely without practice. Only give to any of us, whom you please, an illiterate man to discuss with, and he cannot discover how to deal with the man. But when he has moved the man a little, if he answers beside the purpose, he does not know how to treat him, but he then either abuses or ridicules him, and says, He is an illiterate man; it is not possible to do anything with him. Now a guide, when he has found a man out of the road, leads him into the right way; he does not ridicule or abuse him and then leave him. Do you also show the illiterate man the truth, and you will see that he follows. But so long as you do not show him the truth, do not ridicule him, but rather feel your own incapacity.

Now this was the first and chief peculiarity of Socrates, never to be irritated in argument, never to utter anything abusive, anything insulting, but to bear with abusive persons and to put an end to the quarrel. If you would know what great power he had in this way, read the Symposium of Xenophon, and you will see how many quarrels he put an end to. Hence with good reason in the poets also this power is most highly praised:

Quickly with skill he settles great disputes.
Hesiod, Theogony, v. 87.

ON ANXIETY (SOLICITUDE).—When I see a man anxious, I say, What does this man want? If he did not want something which is not in his power, how could he be anxious? For this reason a lute player when he is singing by himself has no anxiety, but when he enters the theatre, he is anxious, even if he has a good voice and plays well on the lute; for he not only wishes to sing well, but also to obtain applause: but this is not in his power. Accordingly, where he has skill, there he has confidence. Bring any single person who knows nothing of music, and the musician does not care for him. But in the matter where a man knows nothing and has not been practised, there he is anxious. What matter is this? He knows not what a crowd is or what the praise of a crowd is. However, he has learned to strike the lowest chord and the highest; but what the praise of the many is, and what power it has in life, he neither knows nor has he thought about it. Hence he must of necessity tremble and grow pale. Is any man then afraid about things which are not evils? No. Is he afraid about things which are evils, but still so far within his power that they may not happen? Certainly he is not. If then the things which are independent of the will are neither good nor bad, and all things which do depend on the will are within our power, and no man can either take them from us or give them to us, if we do not choose, where is room left for anxiety? But we are anxious about our poor body, our little property, about the will of Cæsar; but not anxious about things internal. Are we anxious about not forming a false opinion? No, for this is in my power. About not exerting our movements contrary to nature? No, not even about this. When then you see a man pale, as the physician says, judging from the complexion, this man's spleen is disordered, that man's liver; so also say, this man's desire and aversion are disordered, he is not in the right way, he is in a fever. For nothing else changes the color, or causes trembling or chattering of the teeth, or causes a man to

Sink in his knees and shift from foot to foot.
Iliad, xiii., 281.

For this reason, when Zeno was going to meet Antigonus, he was not anxious, for Antigonus had no power over any of the things which Zeno admired; and Zeno did not care for those things over which Antigonus had power. But Antigonus was anxious when he was going to meet Zeno, for he wished to please Zeno; but this was a thing external (out of his power). But Zeno did not want to please Antigonus; for no man who is skilled in any art wishes to please one who has no such skill.

Should I try to please you? Why? I suppose, you know the measure by which one man is estimated by another. Have you taken pains to learn what is a good man and what is a bad man, and how a man becomes one or the other? Why then are you not good yourself? How, he replies, am I not good? Because no good man laments or groans or weeps, no good man is pale and trembles, or says, How will he receive me, how will he listen to me? Slave, just as it pleases him. Why do you care about what belongs to others? Is it now his fault if he receives badly what proceeds from you? Certainly. And is it possible that a fault should be one man's, and the evil in another? No. Why then are you anxious about that which belongs to others? Your question is reasonable; but I am anxious how I shall speak to him. Cannot you then speak to him as you choose? But I fear that I may be disconcerted? If you are going to write the name of Dion, are you afraid that you would be disconcerted? By no means. Why? is it not because you have practised writing the name? Certainly. Well, if you were going to read the name, would you not feel the same? and why? Because every art has a certain strength and confidence in the things which belong to it. Have you then not practised speaking? and what else did you learn in the school? Syllogisms and sophistical propositions? For what purpose? was it not for the purpose of discoursing skilfully? and is not discoursing skilfully the same as discoursing seasonably and cautiously and with intelligence, and also without making mistakes and without hindrance, and besides all this with confidence? Yes. When then you are mounted on a horse and go into a plain, are you anxious at being matched against a man who is on foot, and anxious in a matter in which you are practised, and he is not? Yes, but that person (to whom I am going to speak) has power to kill me. Speak the truth, then, unhappy man, and do not brag, nor claim to be a philosopher, nor refuse to acknowledge your masters, but so long as you present this handle in your body, follow every man who is stronger than yourself. Socrates used to practice speaking, he who talked as he did to the tyrants, to the dicasts (judges), he who talked in his prison. Diogenes had practised speaking, he who spoke as he did to Alexander, to the pirates, to the person who bought him. These men were confident in the things which they practised. But do you walk off to your own affairs and never leave them: go and sit in a corner, and weave syllogisms, and propose them to another. There is not in you the man who can rule a state.

TO NASO.—When a certain Roman entered with his son and listened to one reading, Epictetus said, This is the method of instruction; and he stopped. When the Roman asked him to go on, Epictetus said, Every art when it is taught causes labor to him who is unacquainted with it and is unskilled in it, and indeed the things which proceed from the arts immediately show their use in the purpose for which they were made; and most of them contain something attractive and pleasing. For indeed to be present and to observe how a shoemaker learns is not a pleasant thing; but the shoe is useful and also not disagreeable to look at. And the discipline of a smith when he is learning is very disagreeable to one who chances to be present and is a stranger to the art: but the work shows the use of the art. But you will see this much more in music; for if you are present while a person is learning, the discipline will appear most disagreeable; and yet the results of music are pleasing and delightful to those who know nothing of music. And here we conceive the work of a philosopher to be something of this kind: he must adapt his wish ([Greek: boulaesin]) to what is going on, so that neither any of the things which are taking place shall take place contrary to our wish, nor any of the things which do not take place shall not take place when we wish that they should. From this the result is to those who have so arranged the work of philosophy, not to fail in the desire, nor to fall in with that which they would avoid; without uneasiness, without fear, without perturbation to pass through life themselves, together with their associates maintaining the relations both natural and acquired, as the relation of son, of father, of brother, of citizen, of man, of wife, of neighbor, of fellow-traveller, of ruler, of ruled. The work of a philosopher we conceive to be something like this. It remains next to inquire how this must be accomplished.

We see then that the carpenter ([Greek: techton]) when he has learned certain things becomes a carpenter; the pilot by learning certain things becomes a pilot. May it not then in philosophy also not be sufficient to wish to be wise and good, and that there is also a necessity to learn certain things? We inquire then what these things are. The philosophers say that we ought first to learn that there is a God and that he provides for all things; also that it is not possible to conceal from him our acts, or even our intentions and thoughts. The next thing is to learn what is the nature of the gods; for such as they are discovered to be, he, who would please and obey them, must try with all his power to be like them. If the divine is faithful, man also must be faithful; if it is free, man also must be free; if beneficent, man also must be beneficent; if magnanimous, man also must be magnanimous; as being then an imitator of God he must do and say everything consistently with this fact.

TO OR AGAINST THOSE WHO OBSTINATELY PERSIST

IN WHAT THEY HAVE DETERMINED.—When some persons have heard these words, that a man ought to be constant (firm), and that the will is naturally free and not subject to compulsion, but that all other things are subject to hindrance, to slavery, and are in the power of others, they suppose that they ought without deviation to abide by everything which they have determined. But in the first place that which has been determined ought to be sound (true). I require tone (sinews) in the body, but such as exists in a healthy body, in an athletic body; but if it is plain to me that you have the tone of a frenzied man and you boast of it, I shall say to you, Man, seek the physician; this is not tone, but atony (deficiency in right tone). In a different way something of the same kind is felt by those who listen to these discourses in a wrong manner; which was the case with one of my companions, who for no reason resolved to starve himself to death. I heard of it when it was the third day of his abstinence from food, and I went to inquire what had happened. "I have resolved," he said. "But still tell me what it was which induced you to resolve; for if you have resolved rightly, we shall sit with you and assist you to depart, but if you have made an unreasonable resolution, change your mind." "We ought to keep to our determinations." "What are you doing, man? We ought to keep not to all our determinations, but to those which are right; for if you are now persuaded that it is right, do not change your mind, if you think fit, but persist and say, We ought to abide by our determinations. Will you not make the beginning and lay the foundation in an inquiry whether the determination is sound or not sound, and so then build on it firmness and security? But if you lay a rotten and ruinous foundation, will not your miserable little building fall down the sooner, the more and the stronger are the materials which you shall lay on it? Without any reason would you withdraw from us out of life a man who is a friend and a companion, a citizen of the same city, both the great and the small city? Then while you are committing murder and destroying a man who has done no wrong, do you say that you ought to abide by your determinations? And if it ever in any way came into your head to kill me, ought you to abide by your determinations?"

Now this man was with difficulty persuaded to change his mind. But it is impossible to convince some persons at present;

so that I seem now to know what I did not know before, the meaning of the common saying, that you can neither persuade nor break a fool. May it never be my lot to have a wise fool for my friend; nothing is more untractable. "I am determined," the man says. Madmen are also, but the more firmly they form a judgment on things which do not exist, the more hellebore they require. Will you not act like a sick man and call in the physician?—I am sick, master, help me; consider what I must do: it is my duty to obey you. So it is here also: I know not what I ought to do, but I am come to learn.—Not so; but speak to me about other things: upon this I have determined.—What other things? for what is greater and more useful than for you to be persuaded that it is not sufficient to have made your determination and not to change it. This is the tone (energy) of madness, not of health.—I will die, if you compel me to this.—Why, man? What has happened?—I have determined—I have had a lucky escape that you have not determined to kill me—I take no money. Why?—I have determined—Be assured that with the very tone (energy) which you now use in refusing to take, there is nothing to hinder you at some time from inclining without reason to take money, and then saying, I have determined. As in a distempered body, subject to defluxions, the humor inclines sometimes to these parts, and then to those, so too a sickly soul knows not which way to incline; but if to this inclination and movement there is added a tone (obstinate resolution), then the evil becomes past help and cure.

THAT WE DO NOT STRIVE TO USE OUR OPINIONS ABOUT GOOD AND EVIL.—Where is the good? In the will. Where is the evil? In the will. Where is neither of them? In those things which are independent of the will. Well then? Does any one among us think of these lessons out of the schools? Does any one meditate (strive) by himself to give an answer to things as in the case of questions?—Is it day?—Yes.—Is it night?—No.—Well, is the number of stars even?—I cannot say.—When money is shown (offered) to you, have you studied to make the proper answer, that money is not a good thing? Have you practised yourself in these answers, or only against sophisms? Why do you wonder then if in the cases which you have studied, in those you have improved; but in those which you have not studied, in those you remain the same? When the rhetorician knows that he has written well, that he has committed to memory what he has written, and brings an agreeable voice, why is he still anxious? Because he is not satisfied with having studied. What then does he want? To be praised by the audience? For the purpose then of being able to practise declamation he has been disciplined; but with respect to praise and blame he has not been disciplined. For when did he hear from any one what praise is, what blame is, what the nature of each is, what kind of praise should be sought, or what kind of blame should be shunned? And when did he practise this discipline which follows these words (things)? Why then do you still wonder, if in the matters which a man has learned, there he surpasses others, and in those in which he has not been disciplined, there he is the same with the many. So the lute player knows how to play, sings well, and has a fine dress, and yet he trembles when he enters on the stage; for these matters he understands, but he does not know what a crowd is, nor the shouts of a crowd, nor what ridicule is. Neither does he know what anxiety is, whether it is our work or the work of another, whether it is possible to stop it or not. For this reason if he has been praised, he leaves the theatre puffed up, but if he has been ridiculed, the swollen bladder has been punctured and subsides.

This is the case also with ourselves. What do we admire? Externals. About what things are we busy? Externals. And have we any doubt then why we fear or why we are anxious? What then happens when we think the things, which are coming on us, to be evils? It is not in our power not to be afraid, it is not in our power not to be anxious. Then we say, Lord God, how shall I not be anxious? Fool, have you not hands, did not God make them for you? Sit down now and pray that your nose may not run. Wipe yourself rather and do not blame him. Well then, has he given to you nothing in the present case? Has he not given to you endurance? Has he not given to you magnanimity? Has he not given to you manliness? When you have such hands do you still look for one who shall wipe your nose? But we neither study these things nor care for them. Give me a man who cares how he shall do anything, not for the obtaining of a thing, but who cares about his own energy. What man, when he is walking about, cares for his own energy? Who, when he is deliberating, cares about his own deliberation, and not about obtaining that about which he deliberates? And if he succeeds, he is elated and says, How well we have deliberated; did I not tell you, brother, that it is impossible, when we have thought about anything, that it should not turn out thus? But if the thing should turn out otherwise, the wretched man is humbled; he knows not even what to say about what has taken place. Who among us for the sake of this matter has consulted a seer? Who among us as to his actions has not slept in indifference? Who? Give (name) to me one that I may see the man whom I have long been looking for, who is truly noble and ingenuous, whether young or old; name him.

What then are the things which are heavy on us and disturb us? What else than opinions? What else than opinions lies heavy upon him who goes away and leaves his companions and friends and places and habits of life? Now little children, for instance, when they cry on the nurse leaving them for a short time, forget their sorrow if they receive a small cake. Do you choose then that we should compare you to little children? No, by Zeus, for I do not wish to be pacified by a small cake, but by right opinions. And what are these? Such as a man ought to study all day, and not to be affected by anything that is not his own, neither by companion nor place nor gymnasia, and not even by his own body, but to remember the law and to have it before his eyes. And what is the divine law? To keep a man's own, not to claim that which belongs to others, but to use what is given, and when it is not given, not to desire it; and when a thing is taken away, to give it up readily and immediately, and to be thankful for the time that a man has had the use of it, if you would not cry for your nurse and mamma. For what matter does it make by what thing a man is subdued, and on what he depends? In what respect are you better than he who cries for a girl, if you grieve for a little gymnasium, and little porticos, and young men, and such places of amusement? Another comes and laments that he shall no longer drink the water of Dirce. Is the Marcian water worse than that of Dirce? But I was used to the water of Dirce. And you in turn will be used to the other. Then if you become attached to this also, cry for this too, and try to make a verse like the verse of Euripides,

The hot baths of Nero and the Marcian water.

See how tragedy is made when common things happen to silly men.

When then shall I see Athens again and the Acropolis? Wretch, are you not content with what you see daily? Have you anything better or greater to see than the sun, the moon, the stars, the whole earth, the sea? But if indeed you comprehend Him who administers the whole, and carry him about in yourself, do you still desire small stones and a beautiful rock?

HOW WE MUST ADAPT PRECONCEPTIONS TO PARTICULAR CASES.—What is the first business of him who philosophizes? To throw away self-conceit ([Greek: oiaesis]). For it is impossible for a man to begin to learn that which he thinks that he knows. As to things then which ought to be done and ought not to be done, and good and bad, and beautiful and ugly, all of us talking of them at random go to the philosophers; and on these matters we praise, we censure, we accuse, we blame, we judge and determine about principles honorable and dishonorable. But why do we go to the philosophers? Because we wish to learn what we do not think that we know. And what is this? Theorems. For we wish to learn what philosophers say as being something elegant and acute; and some wish to learn that they may get profit from what they learn. It is ridiculous then to think that a person wishes to learn one thing, and will learn another; or further, that a man will make proficiency in that which he does not learn. But the many are deceived by this which deceived also the rhetorician Theopompus, when he blames even Plato for wishing everything to be defined. For what does he say? Did none of us before you use the words good or just, or do we utter the sounds in an unmeaning and empty way without understanding what they severally signify? Now who tells you, Theopompus, that we had not natural notions of each of these things and preconceptions ([Greek: prolaepseis])? But it is not possible to adapt preconceptions to their correspondent objects if we have not distinguished (analyzed) them, and inquired what object must be subjected to each preconception. You may make the same charge against physicians also. For who among us did not use the words healthy and unhealthy before Hippocrates lived, or did we utter these words as empty sounds? For we have also a certain preconception of health, but we are not able to adapt it. For this reason one says, Abstain from food; another says, Give food; another says, Bleed; and another says, Use cupping. What is the reason? is it any other than that a man cannot properly adapt the preconceptions of health to particulars?

HOW WE SHOULD STRUGGLE AGAINST APPEARANCES.—Every habit and faculty is maintained and increased by the corresponding actions: the habit of walking by walking, the habit of running by running. If you would be a good reader, read; if a writer, write. But when you shall not have read for thirty days in succession, but have done something else, you will know the consequence. In the same way, if you shall have lain down ten days, get up and attempt to make a long walk, and you will see how your legs are weakened. Generally then if you would make anything a habit, do it; if you would not make it a habit, do not do it, but accustom yourself to do something else in place of it.

So it is with respect to the affections of the soul: when you have been angry, you must know that not only has this evil befallen you, but that you have also increased the habit, and in a manner thrown fuel upon fire.

In this manner certainly, as philosophers say, also diseases of the mind grow up. For when you have once desired money, if reason be applied to lead to a perception of the evil, the desire is stopped, and the ruling faculty of our mind is restored to the original authority. But if you apply no means of cure, it no longer returns to the same state, but being again excited by the corresponding appearance, it is inflamed to desire quicker than before: and when this takes place continually, it is henceforth hardened (made callous), and the disease of the mind confirms the love of money. For he who has had a fever, and has been relieved from it, is not in the same state that he was before, unless he has been completely cured. Something of the kind happens also in diseases of the soul. Certain traces and blisters are left in it, and unless a man shall completely efface them, when he is again lashed on the same places, the lash will produce not blisters (weals) but sores. If then you wish not to be of an angry temper, do not feed the habit: throw nothing on it which will increase it: at first keep quiet, and count the days on which you have not been angry. I used to be in passion every day; now every second day; then every third, then every fourth. But if you have intermitted thirty days, make a sacrifice to God. For the habit at first begins to be weakened, and then is completely destroyed. "I have not been vexed to-day, nor the day after, nor yet on any succeeding day during two or three months; but I took care when some exciting things happened." Be assured that you are in a good way.

How then shall this be done? Be willing at length to be approved by yourself, be willing to appear beautiful to God, desire to be in purity with your own pure self and with God. Then when any such appearance visits you, Plato says, Have recourse to expiations, go a suppliant to the temples of the averting deities. It is even sufficient if you resort to the society of noble and just men, and compare yourself with them, whether you find one who is living or dead.

But in the first place, be not hurried away by the rapidity of the appearance, but say, Appearances, wait for me a little; let me see who you are, and what you are about; let me put you to the test. And then do not allow the appearance to lead you on and draw lively pictures of the things which will follow; for if you do, it will carry you off wherever it pleases. But rather bring in to oppose it some other beautiful and noble appearance, and cast out this base appearance. And if you are accustomed to be exercised in this way, you will see what shoulders, what sinews, what strength you have. But now it is only trifling words, and nothing more.

This is the true athlete, the man who exercises himself against such appearances. Stay, wretch, do not be carried away. Great is the combat, divine is the work; it is for kingship, for freedom, for happiness, for freedom from perturbation. Remember God; call on him as a helper and protector, as men at sea call on the Dioscuri in a storm. For what is a greater storm than that which comes from appearances which are violent and drive away the reason? For the storm itself, what else is it but an appearance? For take away the fear of death, and suppose as many thunders and lightnings as you please, and you will know what calm and serenity there is in the ruling faculty. But if you have once been defeated and say that you will conquer hereafter, and then say the same again, be assured that you will at last be in so wretched a condition and so weak that you will not even know afterwards that you are doing wrong, but you will even begin to make apologies (defences) for your wrong-doing, and then you will confirm the saying of Hesiod to be true,

With constant ills the dilatory strives.

OF INCONSISTENCY.—Some things men readily confess, and other things they do not. No one then will confess that he is a fool or without understanding; but quite the contrary you will hear all men saying, I wish that I had fortune equal to my understanding. But men readily confess that they are timid, and they say: I am rather timid, I confess; but as to other respects you will not find me to be foolish. A man will not readily confess that he is intemperate; and that he is unjust, he will not confess at all. He will by no means confess that he is envious or a busybody. Most men will confess that they are compassionate. What then is the reason?

The chief thing (the ruling thing) is inconsistency and confusion in the things which relate to good and evil. But different men have different reasons; and generally what they imagine to be base, they do not confess at all. But they suppose timidity to be a characteristic of a good disposition, and compassion also; but silliness to be the absolute characteristic of a slave. And they do not at all admit (confess) the things which are offences against society. But in the case of most errors for this reason chiefly they are induced to confess them, because they imagine that there is something involuntary in them as in timidity and compassion; and if a man confess that he is in any respect intemperate, he alleges love (or passion) as an excuse for what is involuntary. But men do not imagine injustice to be at all involuntary. There is also in jealousy, as they suppose, something involuntary; and for this reason they confess to jealousy also.

Living then among such men, who are so confused, so ignorant of what they say, and of the evils which they have or have not, and why they have them, or how they shall be relieved of them, I think it is worth the trouble for a man to watch constantly (and to ask) whether I also am one of them, what imagination I have about myself, how I conduct myself, whether I conduct myself as a prudent man, whether I conduct myself as a temperate man, whether I ever say this, that I have been taught to be prepared for everything that may happen. Have I the consciousness, which a man who knows nothing ought to have, that I know nothing? Do I go to my teacher as men go to oracles, prepared to obey? or do I like a snivelling boy go to my school to learn history and understand the books which I did not understand before, and, if it should happen so, to explain them also to others? Man, you have had a fight in the house with a poor slave, you have turned the family upside down, you have frightened the neighbors, and you come to me as if you were a wise man, and you take your seat and judge how I have explained some word, and how I have babbled whatever came into my head. You come full of envy, and humbled, because you bring nothing from home; and you sit during the discussion thinking of nothing else than how your father is disposed towards you and your brother. What are they saying about me there? now they think that I am improving, and are saying, He will return with all knowledge. I wish I could learn everything before I return; but much labor is necessary, and no one sends me anything, and the baths at Nicopolis are dirty; everything is bad at home, and bad here.

ON FRIENDSHIP.—What a man applies himself to earnestly, that he naturally loves. Do men then apply themselves earnestly to the things which are bad? By no means. Well, do they apply themselves to things which in no way concern themselves? Not to these either. It remains then that they employ themselves earnestly only about things which are good; and if they are earnestly employed about things, they love such things also. Whoever then understands what is good can also know how to love; but he who cannot distinguish good from bad, and things which are neither good nor bad from both, how can he possess the power of loving? To love, then, is only in the power of the wise.

For universally, be not deceived, every animal is attached to nothing so much as to its own interests. Whatever then appears to it an impediment to this interest, whether this be a brother, or a father, or a child, or beloved, or lover, it hates, spurns, curses; for its nature is to love nothing so much as its own interests: this is father, and brother, and kinsman, and country, and God. When then the gods appear to us to be an impediment to this, we abuse them and throw down their statues and burn their temples, as Alexander ordered the temples of Aesculapius to be burned when his dear friend died.

For this reason, if a man put in the same place his interest, sanctity, goodness, and country, and parents, and friends, all these are secured: but if he puts in one place his interest, in another his friends, and his country and his kinsmen and justice itself, all these give way, being borne down by the weight of interest. For where the I and the Mine are placed, to that place of necessity the animal inclines; if in the flesh, there is the ruling power; if in the will, it is there; and if it is in externals, it is there. If then I am there where my will is, then only shall I be a friend such as I ought to be, and son, and father; for this will be my interest, to maintain the character of fidelity, of modesty, of patience, of abstinence, of active co-operation, of observing my relations (towards all). But if I put myself in one place, and honesty in another, then the doctrine of Epicurus becomes strong, which asserts either that there is no honesty or it is that which opinion holds to be honest (virtuous).

It was through this ignorance that the Athenians and the Lacedaemonians quarrelled, and the Thebans with both; and the great king quarrelled with Hellas, and the Macedonians with both: and the Romans with the Getae. And still earlier the Trojan war happened for these reasons. Alexander was the guest of Menelaus, and if any man had seen their friendly disposition, he would not have believed any one who said that they were not friends. But there was cast between them (as between dogs) a bit of meat, a handsome woman, and about her war arose. And now when you see brothers to be friends appearing to have one mind, do not conclude from this anything about their friendship, not even if they swear it and say that it is impossible for them to be separated from one another. For the ruling principle of a bad man cannot be trusted; it is insecure, has no certain rule by which it is directed, and is overpowered at different times by different appearances. But examine, not what other men examine, if they are born of the same parents and brought up together, and under the same pedagogue; but examine this only, wherein they place their interest, whether in externals or in the will. If in externals, do not name them friends, no more than name them trustworthy or constant, or brave or free; do not name them even men, if you have any judgment. For that is not a principle of human nature which makes them bite one another, and abuse one another, and occupy deserted places or public places, as if they were mountains, and in the courts of justice display the acts of robbers; nor yet that which makes them intemperate and adulterers and corrupters, nor that which makes them do whatever else men do against one another through this one opinion only, that of placing themselves and their interests in the things which are not within the power of their will. But if you hear that in truth these men think the good to be only there, where will is, and where there is a right use of appearances, no longer trouble yourself whether they are father or son, or brothers, or have associated a long time and are companions, but when you have ascertained this only, confidently declare that they are friends, as you declare that they are faithful, that they are just. For where else is friendship than where there is fidelity, and modesty, where there is a communion of honest things and of nothing else.

But you may say, Such a one treated me with regard so long; and did he not love me? How do you know, slave, if he did not regard you in the same way as he wipes his shoes with a sponge, or as he takes care of his beast? How do you know, when you have ceased to be useful as a vessel, he will not throw you away like a broken platter? But this woman is my wife, and we have lived together so long. And how long did Eriphyle live with Amphiaraus, and was the mother of children and of many? But a necklace came between them: and what is a necklace? It is the opinion about such things. That was the bestial principle, that was the thing which broke asunder the friendship between husband and wife, that which did not allow the woman to be a wife nor the mother to be a mother. And let every man among you who has seriously resolved either to be a friend himself or to have another for his friend, cut out these opinions, hate them, drive them from his soul. And thus first of all he will not reproach himself, he will not be at variance with himself, he will not change his mind, he will not torture himself. In the next place, to another also, who is like himself, he will be altogether and completely a friend. But he will bear with the man who is unlike himself, he will be kind to him, gentle, ready to pardon on account of his ignorance, on account of his being mistaken in things of the greatest importance; but he will be harsh to no man, being well convinced of Plato's doctrine that every mind is deprived of truth unwillingly. If you cannot do this, yet you can do in all other respects as friends do, drink together, and lodge together, and sail together, and you may be born of the same parents, for snakes also are: but neither will they be friends, nor you, so long as you retain these bestial and cursed opinions.

ON THE POWER OF SPEAKING.—Every man will read a book with more pleasure or even with more ease, if it is written in fairer characters. Therefore every man will also listen more readily to what is spoken, if it is signified by appropriate and becoming words. We must not say then that there is no faculty of expression: for this affirmation is the characteristic of an impious and also of a timid man. Of an impious man, because he undervalues the gifts which come from God, just as if he would take away the commodity of the power of vision, or hearing, or of seeing. Has then God given you eyes to no purpose? and to no purpose has he infused into them a spirit so strong and of such skilful contrivance as to reach a long way and to fashion the forms of things which are seen? What messenger is so swift and vigilant? And to no purpose has he made the interjacent atmosphere so efficacious and elastic that the vision penetrates through the atmosphere which is in a manner moved? And to no purpose has he made light, without the presence of which there would be no use in any other thing?

Man, be neither ungrateful for these gifts nor yet forget the things which are superior to them. But indeed for the power of seeing and hearing, and indeed for life itself, and for the things which contribute to support it, for the fruits which are dry, and for wine and oil give thanks to God: but remember that he has given you something else better than all these, I mean the power of using them, proving them, and estimating the value of each. For what is that which gives information about each of these powers, what each of them is worth? Is it each faculty itself? Did you ever hear the faculty of vision saying anything about itself? or the faculty of hearing? or wheat, or barley, or a horse, or a dog? No; but they are appointed as ministers and slaves to serve the faculty which has the power of making use of the appearances of things. And if you inquire what is the value of each thing, of whom do you inquire? who answers you? How then can any other faculty be more powerful than this, which uses the rest as ministers and itself proves each and pronounces about them? for which of them knows what itself is, and what is its own value? which of them knows when it ought to employ itself and when not? what faculty is it which opens and closes the eyes, and turns them away from objects to which it ought not to apply them and does apply them to other objects? Is it the faculty of vision? No, but it is the faculty of the will. What is that faculty which closes and opens the ears? what is that by which they are curious and inquisitive, or on the contrary unmoved by what is said? is it the faculty of hearing? It is no other than the faculty of the will. Will this faculty then, seeing that it is amidst all the other faculties which are blind and dumb and unable to see anything else except the very acts for which they are appointed in order to minister to this (faculty) and serve it, but this faculty alone sees sharp and sees what is the value of each of the rest; will this faculty declare to us that anything else is the best, or that itself is? And what else does the eye do when it is opened than see? But whether we ought to look on the wife of a certain person, and in what manner, who tells us? The faculty of the will. And whether we ought to believe what is said or not to believe it, and if we do believe, whether we ought to be moved by it or not, who tells us? Is it not the faculty of the will?

But if you ask me what then is the most excellent of all things, what must I say? I cannot say the power of speaking, but the power of the will, when it is right ([Greek: orthae]). For it is this which uses the other (the power of speaking), and all the other faculties both small and great. For when this faculty of the will is set right, a man who is not good becomes good: but when it fails, a man becomes bad. It is through this that we are unfortunate, that we are fortunate, that we blame one another, are pleased with one another. In a word, it is this which if we neglect it makes unhappiness, and if we carefully look after it, makes happiness.

What then is usually done? Men generally act as a traveller would do on his way to his own country, when he enters a good inn, and being pleased with it should remain there. Man, you have forgotten your purpose: you were not travelling to this inn, but you were passing through it. But this is a pleasant inn. And how many other inns are pleasant? and how many meadows are pleasant? yet only for passing through. But your purpose is this, to return to your country, to relieve your kinsmen of anxiety, to discharge the duties of a citizen, to marry, to beget children, to fill the usual magistracies. For you are not come to select more pleasant places, but to live in these where you were born and of which you were made a citizen. Something of the kind takes place in the matter which we are considering. Since by the aid of speech and such communication as you receive here you must advance to perfection, and purge your will and correct the faculty which makes use of the appearances of things; and since it is necessary also for the teaching (delivery) of theorems to be effected by a certain mode of expression and with a certain variety and sharpness, some persons captivated by these very things abide in them, one captivated by the expression, another by syllogisms, another again by sophisms, and still another by some other inn ([Greek: paudocheiou]) of the kind; and there they stay and waste away as they were among sirens.

Man, your purpose (business) was to make yourself capable of using conformably to nature the appearances presented to you, in your desires not to be frustrated, in your aversion from things not to fall into that which you would avoid, never to have no luck (as one may say), nor ever to have bad luck, to be free, not hindered, not compelled, conforming yourself to the administration of Zeus, obeying it, well satisfied with this, blaming no one, charging no one with fault, able from your whole soul to utter these verses:

Lead me, O Zeus, and thou too Destiny.

TO (OR AGAINST) A PERSON WHO WAS ONE OF THOSE WHO WERE NOT VALUED (ESTEEMED) BY HIM.—A certain person said to him (Epictetus): Frequently I desired to hear you and came to you, and you never gave me any answer; and now, if it is possible, I entreat you to say something to me. Do you think, said Epictetus, that as there is an art in anything else, so there is also an art in speaking, and that he who has the art, will speak skilfully, and he who has not, will speak unskilfully?—I do think so.—He then who by speaking receives benefit himself, and is able to benefit others, will speak skilfully; but he who is rather damaged by speaking and does damage to others, will he be unskilled in this art of speaking? And you may find that some are damaged and others benefited by speaking. And are all who hear benefited by what they hear? Or will you find that among them also some are benefited and some damaged? There are both among these also, he said. In this case also then those who hear skilfully are benefited, and those who hear unskilfully are damaged? He admitted this. Is there then a skill in hearing also, as there is in speaking? It seems so. If you choose, consider the matter in this way also. The practice of music, to whom does it belong? To a musician. And the proper making of a statue, to whom do you think that it belongs? To a statuary. And the looking at a statue skilfully, does this appear to you to require the aid of no art? This also requires the aid of art. Then if speaking properly is the business of the skilful man, do you see that to hear also with benefit is the business of the skilful man? Now as to speaking and hearing perfectly, and usefully, let us for the present, if you please, say no more, for both of us are a long way from everything of the kind. But I think that every man will allow this, that he who is going to hear philosophers requires some amount of practice in hearing. Is it not so?

Why then do you say nothing to me? I can only say this to you, that he who knows not who he is, and for what purpose he exists, and what is this world, and with whom he is associated, and what things are the good and the bad, and the beautiful and the ugly, and who neither understands discourse nor demonstration, nor what is true nor what is false, and who is not able to distinguish them, will neither desire according to nature nor turn away nor move towards, nor intend (to act), nor assent, nor dissent, nor suspend his judgment: to say all in a few words, he will go about dumb and blind, thinking that he is somebody, but being nobody. Is this so now for the first time? Is it not the fact that ever since the human race existed, all errors and misfortunes have arisen through this ignorance?

This is all that I have to say to you; and I say even this not willingly. Why? Because you have not roused me. For what must I look to in order to be roused, as men who are expert in riding are roused by generous horses? Must I look to your body? You treat it disgracefully. To your dress? That is luxurious. To your behavior, to your look? That is the same as nothing. When you would listen to a philosopher, do not say to him, You tell me nothing; but only show yourself worthy of hearing or fit for hearing; and you will see how you will move the speaker.

THAT LOGIC IS NECESSARY.—When one of those who were present said, Persuade me that logic is necessary, he replied, Do you wish me to prove this to you? The answer was, Yes. Then I must use a demonstrative form of speech. This was granted. How then will you know if I am cheating you by my argument? The man was silent. Do you see, said Epictetus, that you yourself are admitting that logic is necessary, if without it you cannot know so much as this, whether logic is necessary or not necessary?

OF FINERY IN DRESS.—A certain young man, a rhetorician, came to see Epictetus, with his hair dressed more carefully than was usual and his attire in an ornamental style; whereupon Epictetus said, Tell me if you do not think that some dogs are beautiful and some horses, and so of all other animals. I do think so, the youth replied. Are not then some men also beautiful and others ugly? Certainly. Do we then for the same reason call each of them in the same kind beautiful, or each beautiful for something peculiar? And you will judge of this matter thus. Since we see a dog naturally formed for one thing, and a horse for another, and for another still, as an example, a nightingale, we may generally and not improperly declare each of them to be beautiful then when it is most excellent according to its nature; but since the nature of each is different, each of them seems to me to be beautiful in a different way. Is it not so? He admitted that it was. That then which makes a dog beautiful, makes a horse ugly; and that which makes a horse beautiful, makes a dog ugly, if it is true that their natures are different. It seems to be so. For I think that what makes a Pancratiast beautiful, makes a wrestler to be not good, and a runner to be most ridiculous; and he who is beautiful for the Pentathlon, is very ugly for wrestling. It is so, said he. What then makes a man beautiful? Is it that which in its kind makes both a dog and a horse beautiful? It is, he said. What then makes a dog beautiful? The possession of the excellence of a dog. And what makes a horse beautiful? The possession of the excellence of a horse. What then makes a man beautiful? Is it not the possession of the excellence of a man? And do you then, if you wish to be beautiful, young man, labor at this, the acquisition of human excellence? But what is this? Observe whom you yourself praise, when you praise many persons without partiality: do you praise the just or the unjust? The just. Whether do you praise the moderate or the immoderate? The moderate. And the temperate or the intemperate? The temperate. If then you make yourself such a person, you will know that you will make yourself beautiful; but so long as you neglect these things, you must be ugly ([Greek: aischron]), even though you contrive all you can to appear beautiful.

IN WHAT A MAN OUGHT TO BE EXERCISED WHO HAS MADE PROFICIENCY; AND THAT WE NEGLECT THE CHIEF THINGS.—There are three things (topics, [Greek: topoi]) in which a man ought to exercise himself who would be wise and good. The first concerns the desires and the aversions, that a man may not fail to get what he desires, and that he may not fall into that which he does not desire. The second concerns the movements towards an object and the movements from an object, and generally in doing what a man ought to do, that he may act according to order, to reason, and not carelessly. The third thing concerns freedom from deception and rashness in judgment, and generally it concerns the assents ([Greek: sugchatatheseis]). Of these topics the chief and the most urgent is that which relates to the affects ([Greek: ta pathae] perturbations); for an affect is produced in no other way than by a failing to obtain that which a man desires or falling into that which a man would wish to avoid. This is that which brings in perturbations, disorders, bad fortune, misfortunes, sorrows, lamentations, and envy; that which makes men envious and jealous; and by these causes we are unable even to listen to the precepts of reason. The second topic concerns the duties of a man; for I ought not to be free from affects ([Greek: apathae]) like a statue, but I ought to maintain the relations ([Greek: scheseis]) natural and acquired, as a pious man, as a son, as a father, as a citizen.

The third topic is that which immediately concerns those who are making proficiency, that which concerns the security of the other two, so that not even in sleep any appearance unexamined may surprise us, nor in intoxication, nor in melancholy. This, it may be said, is above our power. But the present philosophers neglecting the first topic and the second (the affects and duties), employ themselves on the third, using sophistical arguments ([Greek: metapiptontas]), making conclusions from questioning, employing hypotheses, lying. For a man must, it is said, when employed on these matters, take care that he is not deceived. Who must? The wise and good man. This then is all that is wanting to you. Have you successfully worked out the rest? Are you free from deception in the matter of money? If you see a beautiful girl do you resist the appearance? If your neighbor obtains an estate by will, are you not vexed? Now is there nothing else wanting to you except unchangeable firmness of mind ([Greek: ametaptosia])? Wretch, you hear these very things with fear and anxiety that some person may despise you, and with inquiries about what any person may say about you. And if a man come and tell you that in a certain conversation in which the question was, Who is the best philosopher, a man who was present said that a certain person was the chief philosopher, your little soul which was only a finger's length stretches out to two cubits. But if another who is present says, You are mistaken; it is not worth while to listen to a certain person, for what does he know? he has only the first principles, and no more? then you are confounded, you grow pale, you cry out immediately, I will show him who I am, that I am a great philosopher. It is seen by these very things: why do you wish to show it by others? Do you not know that Diogenes pointed out one of the sophists in this way by stretching out his middle finger? And then when the man was wild with rage, This, he said, is the certain person: I have pointed him out to you. For a man is not shown by the finger, as a stone or a piece of wood; but when any person shows the man's principles, then he shows him as a man.

Let us look at your principles also. For is it not plain that you value not at all your own will ([Greek: proairesis]), but you look externally to things which are independent of your will? For instance, what will a certain person say? and what will people think of you? Will you be considered a man of learning; have you read Chrysippus or Antipater? for if you have read Archedamus also, you have every thing (that you can desire). Why you are still uneasy lest you should not show us who you are? Would you let me tell you what manner of man you have shown us that you are? You have exhibited yourself to us as a mean fellow, querulous, passionate, cowardly, finding fault with everything, blaming everybody, never quiet, vain: this is what you have exhibited to us. Go away now and read Archedamus; then if a mouse should leap down and make a noise, you are a dead man. For such a death awaits you as it did—what was the man's name—Crinis; and he too was proud, because he understood Archedamus. Wretch, will you not dismiss these things that do not concern you at all? These things are suitable to those who are able to learn them without perturbation, to those who can say: "I am not subject to anger, to grief, to envy: I am not hindered, I am not restrained. What remains for me? I have leisure, I am tranquil: let us see how we must deal with sophistical arguments; let us see how when a man has accepted an hypothesis he shall not be led away to any thing absurd." To them such things belong. To those who are happy it is appropriate to light a fire, to dine; if they choose, both to sing and to dance. But when the vessel is sinking, you come to me and hoist the sails.

WHAT IS THE MATTER ON WHICH A GOOD MAN

SHOULD BE EMPLOYED, AND IN WHAT WE OUGHT CHIEFLY TO PRACTISE OURSELVES.—The material for the wise and good man is his own ruling faculty: and the body is the material for the physician and the aliptes (the man who oils persons); the land is the matter for the husbandman. The business of the wise and good man is to use appearances conformably to nature: and as it is the nature of every soul to assent to the truth, to dissent from the false, and to remain in suspense as to that which is uncertain; so it is its nature to be moved towards the desire for the good, and to aversion from the evil; and with respect to that which is neither good nor bad it feels indifferent. For as the money-changer (banker) is not allowed to reject Cæsar's coin, nor the seller of herbs, but if you show the coin, whether he chooses or not, he must give up what is sold for the coin; so it is also in the matter of the soul. When the good appears, it immediately attracts to itself; the evil repels from itself. But the soul will never reject the manifest appearance of the good, any more than persons will reject Cæsar's coin. On this principle depends every movement both of man and God.

Against (or with respect to) this kind of thing chiefly a man should exercise himself. As soon as you go out in the morning, examine every man whom you see, every man whom you hear; answer as to a question, What have you seen? A handsome man or woman? Apply the rule. Is this independent of the will, or dependent? Independent. Take it away. What have you seen? A man lamenting over the death of a child. Apply the rule. Death is a thing independent of the will. Take it away. Has the proconsul met you? Apply the rule. What kind of a thing is a proconsul's office? Independent of the will or dependent on it? Independent. Take this away also; it does not stand examination; cast it away; it is nothing to you.

If we practised this and exercised ourselves in it daily from morning to night, something indeed would be done. But now we are forthwith caught half asleep by every appearance, and it is only, if ever, that in the school we are roused a little. Then when we go out, if we see a man lamenting, we say, He is undone. If we see a consul, we say, He is happy. If we see an exiled man, we say, He is miserable. If we see a poor man, we say, He is wretched; he has nothing to eat.

We ought then to eradicate these bad opinions, and to this end we should direct all our efforts. For what is weeping and lamenting? Opinion. What is bad fortune? Opinion. What is civil sedition, what is divided opinion, what is blame, what is accusation, what is impiety, what is trifling? All these things are opinions, and nothing more, and opinions about things independent of the will, as if they were good and bad. Let a man transfer these opinions to things dependent on the will, and I engage for him that he will be firm and constant, whatever may be the state of things around him. Such as is a dish of water, such is the soul. Such as is the ray of light which falls on the water, such are the appearances. When the water is moved, the ray also seems to be moved, yet it is not moved. And when then a man is seized with giddiness, it is not the arts and the virtues which are confounded, but the spirit (the nervous power) on which they are impressed; but if the spirit be restored to its settled state, those things also are restored.

MISCELLANEOUS.—When some person asked him how it happened that since reason has been more cultivated by the men of the present age, the progress made in former times was greater. In what respect, he answered, has it been more cultivated now, and in what respect was the progress greater then? For in that in which it has now been more cultivated, in that also the progress will now be found. At present it has been cultivated for the purpose of resolving syllogisms, and progress is made. But in former times it was cultivated for the purpose of maintaining the governing faculty in a condition conformable to nature, and progress was made. Do not then mix things which are different, and do not expect, when you are laboring at one thing to make progress in another. But see if any man among us when he is intent upon this, the keeping himself in a state conformable to nature and living so always, does not make progress. For you will not find such a man.

It is not easy to exhort weak young men; for neither is it easy to hold (soft) cheese with a hook. But those who have a good natural disposition, even if you try to turn them aside, cling still more to reason.

TO THE ADMINISTRATOR OF THE FREE CITIES WHO WAS AN EPICUREAN.—When the administrator came to visit him, and the man was an Epicurean, Epictetus said, It is proper for us who are not philosophers to inquire of you who are philosophers, as those who come to a strange city inquire of the citizens and those who are acquainted with it, what is the best thing in the world, in order that we also after inquiry may go in quest of that which is best and look at it, as strangers do with the things in cities. For that there are three things which relate to man—soul, body, and things external, scarcely any man denies. It remains for you philosophers to answer what is the best. What shall we say to men? Is the flesh the best? and was it for this that Maximus sailed as far as Cassiope in winter (or bad weather) with his son, and accompanied him that he might be gratified in the flesh? When the man said that it was not, and added, Far be that from him. Is it not fit then, Epictetus said, to be actively employed about the best? It is certainly of all things the most fit. What then do we possess which is better than the flesh? The soul, he replied. And the good things of the best, are they better, or the good things of the worse? The good things of the best. And are the good things of the best within the power of the will or not within the power of the will? They are within the power of the will. Is then the pleasure of the soul a thing within the power of the will? It is, he replied. And on what shall this pleasure depend? On itself? But that cannot be conceived; for there must first exist a certain substance or nature ([Greek: ousia]) of good, by obtaining which we shall have pleasure in the soul. He assented to this also. On what then shall we depend for this pleasure of the soul? for if it shall depend on things of the soul, the substance (nature) of the good is discovered; for good cannot be one thing, and that at which we are rationally delighted another thing; nor if that which precedes is not good, can that which comes after be good, for in order that the thing which comes after may be good, that which precedes must be good. But you would not affirm this, if you are in your right mind, for you would then say what is inconsistent both with Epicurus and the rest of your doctrines. It remains then that the pleasure of the soul is in the pleasure from things of the body; and again that those bodily things must be the things which precede and the substance (nature) of the good.

Seek for doctrines which are consistent with what I say, and by making them your guide you will with pleasure abstain from things which have such persuasive power to lead us and overpower us. But if to the persuasive power of these things, we also devise such a philosophy as this which helps to push us on towards them and strengthens us to this end, what will be the consequence? In a piece of toreutic art which is the best part? the silver or the workmanship? The substance of the hand is the flesh; but the work of the hand is the principal part (that which precedes and leads the rest). The duties then are also three: those which are directed towards the existence of a thing; those which are directed towards its existence in a particular kind; and third, the chief or leading things themselves. So also in man we ought not to value the material, the poor flesh, but the principal (leading things, [Greek: ta proaegoumena]). What are these? Engaging in public business, marrying, begetting children, venerating God, taking care of parents, and generally, having desires, aversions ([Greek: echchlinein]), pursuits of things and avoidances, in the way in which we ought to do these things, and according to our nature. And how are we constituted by nature? Free, noble, modest; for what other animal blushes? what other is capable of receiving the appearance (the impression) of shame? and we are so constituted by nature as to subject pleasure to these things, as a minister, a servant, in order that it may call forth our activity, in order that it may keep us constant in acts which are conformable to nature.

HOW WE MUST EXERCISE OURSELVES AGAINST APPEARANCES ([Greek: phantasias]).—As we exercise ourselves against sophistical questions, so we ought to exercise ourselves daily against appearances; for these appearances also propose questions to us. A certain person's son is dead. Answer; the thing is not within the power of the will: it is not an evil. A father has disinherited a certain son. What do you think of it? It is a thing beyond the power of the will, not an evil. Cæsar has condemned a person. It is a thing beyond the power of the will, not an evil. The man is afflicted at this. Affliction is a thing which depends on the will: it is an evil. He has borne the condemnation bravely. That is a thing within the power of the will: it is a good. If we train ourselves in this manner, we shall make progress; for we shall never assent to anything of which there is not an appearance capable of being comprehended. Your son is dead. What has happened? Your son is dead. Nothing more? Nothing. Your ship is lost. What has happened? Your ship is lost. A man has been led to prison. What has happened? He has been led to prison. But that herein he has fared badly, every man adds from his own opinion. But Zeus, you say, does not do right in these matters. Why? because he has made you capable of endurance? because he has made you magnanimous? because he has taken from that which befalls you the power of being evils? because it is in your power to be happy while you are suffering what you suffer? because he has opened the door to you, when things do not please you? Man, go out and do not complain!

Hear how the Romans feel towards philosophers, if you would like to know. Italicus, who was the most in repute of the philosophers, once when I was present, being vexed with his own friends and as if he was suffering something intolerable, said: "I cannot bear it, you are killing me; you will make me such as that man is," pointing to me.

TO A CERTAIN RHETORICIAN WHO WAS GOING UP TO ROME ON A SUIT.—When a certain person came to him, who was going up to Rome on account of a suit which had regard to his rank, Epictetus inquired the reason of his going to Rome, and the man then asked what he thought about the matter. Epictetus replied: If you ask me what you will do in Rome, whether you will succeed or fail, I have no rule ([Greek: theoraema]) about this. But if you ask me how you will fare, I can tell you: if you have right opinions ([Greek: dogmata]), you will fare well; if they are false, you will fare ill. For to every man the cause of his acting is opinion. For what is the reason why you desired to be elected governor of the Cnossians? Your opinion. What is the reason that you are now going up to Rome? Your opinion. And going in winter, and with danger and expense? I must go. What tells you this? Your opinion. Then if opinions are the causes of all actions, and a man has bad opinions, such as the cause may be, such also is the effect! Have we then all sound opinions, both you and your adversary? And how do you differ? But have you sounder opinions than your adversary? Why? You think so. And so does he think that his opinions are better; and so do madmen. This is a bad criterion. But show to me that you have made some inquiry into your opinions and have taken some pains about them. And as now you are sailing to Rome in order to become governor of the Cnossians, and you are not content to stay at home with the honors which you had, but you desire something greater and more conspicuous, so when did you ever make a voyage for the purpose of examining your own opinions, and casting them out, if you have any that are bad? Whom have you approached for this purpose? What time have you fixed for it? What age? Go over the times of your life by yourself, if you are ashamed of me (knowing the fact) when you were a boy, did you examine your own opinions? and did you not then, as you do all things now, do as you did do? and when you were become a youth and attended the rhetoricians, and yourself practised rhetoric, what did you imagine that you were deficient in? And when you were a young man and engaged in public matters, and pleaded causes yourself, and were gaining reputation, who then seemed your equal? And when would you have submitted to any man examining and showing that your opinions are bad? What then do you wish me to say to you? Help me in this matter. I have no theorem (rule) for this. Nor have you, if you came to me for this purpose, come to me as a philosopher, but as to a seller of vegetables or a shoemaker. For what purpose then have philosophers theorems? For this purpose, that whatever may happen, our ruling faculty may be and continue to be conformable to nature. Does this seem to you a small thing? No; but the greatest. What then? does it need only a short time? and is it possible to seize it as you pass by? If you can, seize it.

Then you will say, I met with Epictetus as I should meet with a stone or a statue: for you saw me and nothing more. But he meets with a man as a man, who learns his opinions, and in his turn shows his own. Learn my opinions: show me yours; and then say that you have visited me. Let us examine one another: if I have any bad opinion, take it away; if you have any, show it. This is the meaning of meeting with a philosopher. Not so (you say): but this is only a passing visit, and while we are hiring the vessel, we can also see Epictetus. Let us see what he says. Then you go away and say: Epictetus was nothing; he used solecisms and spoke in a barbarous way. For of what else do you come as judges? Well, but a man may say to me, if I attend to such matters (as you do), I shall have no land as you have none; I shall have no silver cups as you have none, nor fine beasts as you have none. In answer to tins it is perhaps sufficient to say: I have no need of such things; but if you possess many things you have need of others: whether you choose or not, you are poorer than I am. What then have I need of? Of that which you have not? of firmness, of a mind which is conformable to nature, of being free from perturbation.

IN WHAT MANNER WE OUGHT TO BEAR SICKNESS.— When the need of each opinion comes, we ought to have it in readiness: on the occasion of breakfast, such opinions as relate to breakfast; in the bath, those that concern the bath; in bed, those that concern bed.

> Let sleep not come upon thy languid eyes
> Before each daily action thou hast scann'd;
> What's done amiss, what done, what left undone;
> From first to last examine all, and then
> Blame what is wrong, in what is right rejoice.

And we ought to retain these verses in such way that we may use them, not that we may utter them aloud, as when we exclaim, "Paean Apollo." Again in fever we should have ready such opinions as concern a fever; and we ought not, as soon as the fever begins, to lose and forget all. A man who has a fever may say: If I philosophize any longer, may I be hanged: wherever I go, I must take care of the poor body, that a fever may not come. But what is philosophizing? Is it not a preparation against events which may happen? Do you not understand that you are saying something of this kind? "If I shall still prepare myself to bear with patience what happens, may I be hanged." But this is just as if a man after receiving blows should give up the Pancratium. In the Pancratium it is in our power to desist and not to receive blows.

But in the other matter if we give up philosophy, what shall we gain? What then should a man say on the occasion of each painful thing? It was for this that I exercised myself, for this I disciplined myself. God says to you: Give me a proof that you have duly practised athletics, that you have eaten what you ought, that you have been exercised, that you have obeyed the aliptes (the oiler and rubber). Then do you show yourself weak when the time for action comes? Now is the time for the fever. Let it be borne well. Now is the time for thirst, bear it well. Now is the time for hunger, bear it well. Is it not in your power? Who shall hinder you? The physician will hinder you from drinking; but he cannot prevent you from bearing thirst well: and he will hinder you from eating; but he cannot prevent you from bearing hunger well.

But I cannot attend to my philosophical studies. And for what purpose do you follow them? Slave, is it not that you may be happy, that you may be constant, is it not that you may be in a state conformable to nature and live so? What hinders you when you have a fever from having your ruling faculty conformable to nature? Here is the proof of the thing, here is the test of the philosopher. For this also is a part of life, like walking, like sailing, like journeying by land, so also is fever. Do you read when you are walking? No. Nor do you when you have a fever. But if you walk about well, you have all that belongs to a man who walks. If you bear a fever well, you have all that belongs to a man in a fever. What is it to bear a fever well? Not to blame God or man; not to be afflicted at that which happens, to expect death well and nobly, to do what must be done: when the physician comes in, not to be frightened at what he says; nor if he says you are doing well, to be overjoyed. For what good has he told you? and when you were in health, what good was that to you? And even if he says you are in a bad way, do not despond. For what is it to be ill? is it that you are near the severance of the soul and the body? what harm is there in this? If you are not near now, will you not afterwards be near? Is the world going to be turned upside down when you are dead? Why then do you flatter the physician? Why do you say if you please, master, I shall be well? Why do you give him an opportunity of raising his eyebrows (being proud; or showing his importance)? Do you not value a physician, as you do a shoemaker when he is measuring your foot, or a carpenter when he is building your house, and so treat the physician as to the body which is not yours, but by nature dead? He who has a fever has an opportunity of doing this: if he does these things, he has what belongs to him. For it is not the business of a philosopher to look after these externals, neither his wine nor his oil nor his poor body, but his own ruling power. But as to externals how must he act? so far as not to be careless about them. Where then is there reason for fear? where is there then still reason for anger, and of fear about what belongs to others, about things which are of no value? For we ought to have these two principles in readiness, that except the will nothing is good nor bad; and that we ought not to lead events, but to follow them. My brother ought not to have behaved thus to me. No, but he will see to that; and, however he may behave, I will conduct myself towards him as I ought. For this is my own business; that belongs to another: no man can prevent this, the other thing can be hindered.

ABOUT EXERCISE.—We ought not to make our exercises consist in means contrary to nature and adapted to cause admiration, for if we do so, we who call ourselves philosophers, shall not differ at all from jugglers. For it is difficult even to walk on a rope; and not only difficult, but it is also dangerous. Ought we for this reason to practice walking on a rope, or setting up a palm-tree, or embracing statues? By no means. Every thing which is difficult and dangerous is not suitable for practice; but that is suitable which conduces to the working out of that which is proposed to us. And what is that which is proposed to us as a thing to be worked out? To live with desire and aversion (avoidance of certain things) free from restraint. And what is this? Neither to be disappointed in that which you desire, nor to fall into anything which you would avoid. Towards this object then exercise (practice) ought to tend. For since it is not possible to have your desire not disappointed and your aversion free from falling into that which you would avoid, without great and constant practice, you must know that if you allow your desire and aversion to turn to things which are not within the power of the will, you will neither have your desire capable of attaining your object, nor your aversion free from the power of avoiding that which you would avoid. And since strong habit leads (prevails), and we are accustomed to employ desire and aversion only to things which are not within the power of our will, we ought to oppose to this habit a contrary habit, and where there is great slipperiness in the appearances, there to oppose the habit of exercise. Then at last, if occasion presents itself, for the purpose of trying yourself at a proper time you will descend into the arena to know if appearances overpower you as they did formerly. But at first fly far from that which is stronger than yourself; the contest is unequal between a charming young girl and a beginner in philosophy. The earthen pitcher, as the saying is, and the rock do not agree.

WHAT SOLITUDE IS, AND WHAT KIND OF PERSON A SOLITARY MAN IS.—Solitude is a certain condition of a helpless man. For because a man is alone, he is not for that reason also solitary; just as though a man is among numbers, he is not therefore not solitary. When then we have lost either a brother, or a son, or a friend on whom we were accustomed to repose, we say that we are left solitary, though we are often in Rome, though such a crowd meet us, though so many live in the same place, and sometimes we have a great number of slaves. For the man who is solitary, as it is conceived, is considered to be a helpless person and exposed to those who wish to harm him. For this reason when we travel, then especially do we say that we are lonely when we fall among robbers, for it is not the sight of a human creature which removes us from solitude, but the sight of one who is faithful and modest and helpful to us. For if being alone is enough to make solitude, you may say that even Zeus is solitary in the conflagration and bewails himself saying, Unhappy that I am who have neither Hera, nor Athena, nor Apollo, nor brother, nor son, nor descendant, nor kinsman. This is what some say that he does when he is alone at the conflagration. For they do not understand how a man passes his life when he is alone, because they set out from a certain natural principle, from the natural desire of community and mutual love and from the pleasure of conversation among men. But none the less a man ought to be prepared in a manner for this also (being alone), to be able to be sufficient for himself and to be his own companion. For as Zeus dwells with himself, and is tranquil by himself, and thinks of his own administration and of its nature, and is employed in thoughts suitable to himself; so ought we also to be able to talk with ourselves, not to feel the want of others also, not to be unprovided with the means of passing our time; to observe the divine administration, and the relation of ourselves to everything else; to consider how we formerly were affected towards things that happened and how at present; what are still the things which give us pain; how these also can be cured and how removed; if any things require improvement, to improve them according to reason.

Well then, if some man should come upon me when I am alone and murder me? Fool, not murder You, but your poor body.

What kind of solitude then remains? what want? why do we make ourselves worse than children; and what do children do when they are left alone? They take up shells and ashes, and they build something, then pull it down, and build something else, and so they never want the means of passing the time. Shall I then, if you sail away, sit down and weep, because I have been left alone and solitary? Shall I then have no shells, no ashes? But children do what they do through want of thought (or deficiency in knowledge), and we through knowledge are unhappy.

Every great power (faculty) is dangerous to beginners. You must then bear such things as you are able, but conformably to nature: but not ... Practise sometimes a way of living like a person out of health that you may at some time live like a man in health.

CERTAIN MISCELLANEOUS MATTERS.—As bad tragic actors cannot sing alone, but in company with many, so some persons cannot walk about alone. Man, if you are anything, both walk alone and talk to yourself, and do not hide yourself in the chorus. Examine a little at last, look around, stir yourself up, that you may know who you are.

You must root out of men these two things, arrogance (pride) and distrust. Arrogance then is the opinion that you want nothing (are deficient in nothing); but distrust is the opinion that you cannot be happy when so many circumstances surround you. Arrogance is removed by confutation; and Socrates was the first who practised this. And (to know) that the thing is not impossible inquire and seek. This search will do you no harm; and in a manner this is philosophizing, to seek how it is possible to employ desire and aversion ([Greek: echchlisis]) without impediment.

I am superior to you, for my father is a man of consular rank. Another says, I have been a tribune, but you have not. If we were horses, would you say, My father was swifter? I have much barley and fodder, or elegant neck ornaments. If then you were saying this, I said, Be it so: let us run then. Well, is there nothing in a man such as running in a horse, by which it will be known which is superior and inferior? Is there not modesty ([Greek: aidos]), fidelity, justice? Show yourself superior in these, that you may be superior as a man. If you tell me that you can kick violently, I also will say to you, that you are proud of that which is the act of an ass.

THAT WE OUGHT TO PROCEED WITH CIRCUMSPECTION TO EVERYTHING.[Footnote: Compare Encheiridion, 29.]—In every act consider what precedes and what follows, and then proceed to the act. If you do not consider, you will at first begin with spirit, since you have not thought at all of the things which follow; but afterwards when some consequences have shown themselves, you will basely desist (from that which you have begun).—I wish to conquer at the Olympic games.—(And I too, by the gods; for it is a fine thing.) But consider here what precedes and what follows; and then, if it is for your good, undertake the thing. You must act according to rules, follow strict diet, abstain from delicacies, exercise yourself by compulsion at fixed times, in heat, in cold; drink no cold water, nor wine, when there is opportunity of drinking it. In a word, you must surrender yourself to the trainer, as you do to a physician. Next in the contest, you must be covered with sand, sometimes dislocate a hand, sprain an ankle, swallow a quantity of dust, be scourged with the whip; and after undergoing all this, you must sometimes be conquered. After reckoning all these things, if you have still an inclination, go to the athletic practice. If you do not reckon them, observe you will behave like children who at one time play as wrestlers, then as gladiators, then blow a trumpet, then act a tragedy, when they have seen and admired such things. So you also do: you are at one time a wrestler (athlete), then a gladiator, then a philosopher, then a rhetorician; but with your whole soul you are nothing: like the ape you imitate all that you see; and always one thing after another pleases you, but that which becomes familiar displeases you. For you have never undertaken anything after consideration, nor after having explored the whole matter and put it to a strict examination; but you have undertaken it at hazard and with a cold desire. Thus some persons having seen a philosopher and having heard one speak like Euphrates—and yet who can speak like him?—wish to be philosophers themselves.

Man, consider first what the matter is (which you propose to do), then your own nature also, what it is able to bear. If you are a wrestler, look at your shoulders, your thighs, your loins: for different men are naturally formed for different things. Do you think that, if you do (what you are doing daily), you can be a philosopher? Do you think that you can eat as you do now, drink as you do now, and in the same way be angry and out of humor? You must watch, labor, conquer certain desires, you must depart from your kinsmen, be despised by your slaves, laughed at by those who meet you, in everything you must be in an inferior condition, as to magisterial office, in honors, in courts of justice. When you have considered all these things completely, then, if you think proper, approach to philosophy, if you would gain in exchange for these things freedom from perturbations, liberty, tranquillity. If you have not considered these things, do not approach philosophy: do not act like children, at one time a philosopher, then a tax collector, then a rhetorician, then a procurator (officer) of Cæsar. These things are not consistent. You must be one man either good or bad; you must either labor at your own ruling faculty or at external things; you must either labor at things within or at external things; that is, you must either occupy the place of a philosopher or that of one of the vulgar.

A person said to Rufus when Galba was murdered: Is the world now governed by Providence? But Rufus replied: Did I ever incidentally form an argument from Galba that the world is governed by Providence?

THAT WE OUGHT WITH CAUTION TO ENTER INTO FAMILIAR INTERCOURSE WITH MEN.

—If a man has frequent intercourse with others either for talk, or drinking together, or generally for social purposes, he must either become like them, or change them to his own fashion. For if a man places a piece of quenched charcoal close to a piece that is burning, either the quenched charcoal will quench the other, or the burning charcoal will light that which is quenched. Since then the danger is so great, we must cautiously enter into such intimacies with those of the common sort, and remember that it is impossible that a man can keep company with one who is covered with soot without being partaker of the soot himself. For what will you do if a man speaks about gladiators, about horses, about athletes, or what is worse about men? Such a person is bad, such a person is good; this was well done, this was done badly. Further, if he scoff, or ridicule, or show an ill-natured disposition? Is any man among us prepared like a lute-player when he takes a lute, so that as soon as he has touched the strings, he discovers which are discordant, and tunes the instrument? Such a power as Socrates had who in all his social intercourse could lead his companions to his own purpose? How should you have this power? It is therefore a necessary consequence that you are carried about by the common kind of people.

Why then are they more powerful than you? Because they utter these useless words from their real opinions; but you utter your elegant words only from your lips; for this reason they are without strength and dead, and it is nauseous to listen to your exhortations and your miserable virtue, which is talked of everywhere (up and down). In this way the vulgar have the advantage over you; for every opinion ([Greek: dogma]) is strong and invincible. Until then the good ([Greek: chompsai]) sentiments ([Greek: hupolaepseis]) are fixed in you, and you shall have acquired a certain power for your security, I advise you to be careful in your association with common persons; if you are not, every day like wax in the sun there will be melted away whatever you inscribe on your minds in the school. Withdraw then yourselves far from the sun so long as you have these waxen sentiments. For this reason also philosophers advise men to leave their native country, because ancient habits distract them and do not allow a beginning to be made of a different habit; nor can we tolerate those who meet us and say: See such a one is now a philosopher, who was once so and so. Thus also physicians send those who have lingering diseases to a different country and a different air; and they do right. Do you also introduce other habits than those which you have; fix you opinions and exercise yourselves in them. But you do not so; you go hence to a spectacle, to a show of gladiators, to a place of exercise ([Greek: chuston]), to a circus; then you come back hither, and again from this place you go to those places, and still the same persons. And there is no pleasing (good) habit, nor attention, nor care about self and observation of this kind. How shall I use the appearances presented to me? according to nature, or contrary to nature? how do I answer to them? as I ought, or as I ought not? Do I say to those things which are independent of the will, that they do not concern me? For if you are not yet in this state, fly from your former habits, fly from the common sort, if you intend ever to begin to be something.

ON PROVIDENCE.-When you make any charge against Providence, consider, and you will learn that the thing has happened according to reason. Yes, but the unjust man has the advantage. In what? In money. Yes, for he is superior to you in this, that he flatters, is free from shame, and is watchful. What is the wonder? But see if he has the advantage over you in being faithful, in being modest; for you will not find it to be so; but wherein you are superior, there you will find that you have the advantage. And I once said to a man who was vexed because Philostorgus was fortunate: Would you choose to lie with Sura? May it never happen, he replied, that this day should come? Why then are you vexed, if he receives something in return for that which he sells; or how can you consider him happy who acquires those things by such means as you abominate; or what wrong does Providence, if he gives the better things to the better men? Is it not better to be modest than to be rich? He admitted this. Why are you vexed then, man, when you possess the better thing? Remember then always and have in readiness the truth, that this is a law of nature, that the superior has an advantage over the inferior in that in which he is superior; and you will never be vexed.

But my wife treats me badly. Well, if any man asks you what this is, say, my wife treats me badly. Is there then nothing more? Nothing. My father gives me nothing. (What is this? my father gives me nothing. Is there nothing else then? Nothing); but to say that this is an evil is something which must be added to it externally, and falsely added. For this reason we must not get rid of poverty, but of the opinion about poverty, and then we shall be happy.

ABOUT CYNICISM.—When one of his pupils inquired of Epictetus, and he was a person who appeared to be inclined to Cynicism, what kind of person a Cynic ought to be, and what was the notion ([Greek: prolaepsis]) of the thing, we will inquire, said Epictetus, at leisure; but I have so much to say to you that he who without God attempts so great a matter, is hateful to God, and has no other purpose than to act indecently in public.

In the first place, in the things which relate to yourself, you must not be in any respect like what you do now; you must not blame God or man; you must take away desire altogether, you must transfer avoidance ([Greek: echchlisis]) only to the things which are within the power of the will; you must not feel anger nor resentment or envy nor pity; a girl must not appear handsome to you, nor must you love a little reputation, nor be pleased with a boy or a cake. For you ought to know that the rest of men throw walls around them and houses and darkness when they do any such things, and they have many means of concealment. A man shuts the door, he sets somebody before the chamber; if a person comes, say that he is out, he is not at leisure. But the Cynic instead of all these things must use modesty as his protection; if he does not, he will be indecent in his nakedness and under the open sky. This is his house, his door; this is the slave before his bedchamber; this is his darkness. For he ought not to wish to hide anything that he does; and if he does, he is gone, he has lost the character of a Cynic, of a man who lives under the open sky, of a free man; he has begun to fear some external thing, he has begun to have need of concealment, nor can he get concealment when he chooses. For where shall he hide himself and how? And if by chance this public instructor shall be detected, this pædagogue, what kind of things will he be compelled to suffer? when then a man fears these things, is it possible for him to be bold with his whole soul to superintend men? It cannot be: it is impossible.

In the first place then you must make your ruling faculty pure, and this mode of life also. Now (you should say), to me the matter to work on is my understanding, as wood is to the carpenter, as hides to the shoemaker; and my business is the right use of appearances. But the body is nothing to me: the parts of it are nothing to me. Death? Let it come when it chooses, either death of the whole or of a part. Fly, you say. And whither; can any man eject me out of the world? He cannot. But wherever I go, there is the sun, there is the moon, there are the stars, dreams, omens, and the conversation ([Greek: omilia]) with gods.

Then, if he is thus prepared, the true Cynic cannot be satisfied with this; but he must know that he is sent a messenger from Zeus to men about good and bad things, to show them that they have wandered and are seeking the substance of good and evil where it is not, but where it is, they never think; and that he is a spy, as Diogenes was carried off to Philip after the battle of Chaeroneia as a spy. For in fact a Cynic is a spy of the things which are good for men and which are evil, and it is his duty to examine carefully and to come and report truly, and not to be struck with terror so as to point out as enemies those who are not enemies, nor in any other way to be perturbed by appearances nor confounded.

It is his duty then to be able with a loud voice, if the occasion should arise, and appearing on the tragic stage to say like Socrates: Men, whither are you hurrying, what are you doing, wretches? like blind people you are wandering up and down; you are going by another road, and have left the true road; you seek for prosperity and happiness where they are not, and if another shows you where they are, you do not believe him. Why do you seek it without? In the body? It is not there. If you doubt, look at Myro, look at Ophellius. In possessions? It is not there. But if you do not believe me, look at Croesus: look at those who are now rich, with what lamentations their life is filled. In power? It is not there. If it is, those must be happy who have been twice and thrice consuls; but they are not. Whom shall we believe in these matters? You who from without see their affairs and are dazzled by an appearance, or the men themselves? What do they say? Hear them when they groan, when they grieve, when on account of these very consulships and glory and splendor they think that they are more wretched and in greater danger. Is it in royal power? It is not: if it were, Nero would have been happy, and Sardanapalus. But neither was Agamemnon happy, though he was a better man than Sardanapalus and Nero; but while others are snoring, what is he doing?

> Much from his head he tore his rooted hair:
> Iliad, x., 15.

and what does he say himself?

> "I am perplexed," he says, "and
> Disturb'd I am," and "my heart out of my bosom
> Is leaping."
> Iliad, x., 91.

Wretch, which of your affairs goes badly? Your possessions? No. Your body? No. But you are rich in gold and copper. What then is the matter with you? That part of you, whatever it is, has been neglected by you and is corrupted, the part with which we desire, with which we avoid, with which we move towards and move from things. How neglected? He knows not the nature of good for which he is made by nature and the nature of evil; and what is his own, and what belongs to another; and when anything that belongs to others goes badly, he says, Woe to me, for the Hellenes are in danger. Wretched is his ruling faculty, and alone neglected and uncared for. The Hellenes are going to die destroyed by the Trojans. And if the Trojans do not kill them, will they not die? Yes; but not all at once. What difference then does it make? For if death is an evil, whether men die altogether, or if they die singly, it is equally an evil. Is anything else then going to happen than the separation of the soul and the body?

Nothing. And if the Hellenes perish, is the door closed, and is it not in your power to die? It is. Why then do you lament (and say), Oh, you are a king and have the sceptre of Zeus? An unhappy king does not exist more than an unhappy god. What then art thou? In truth a shepherd: for you weep as shepherds do, when a wolf has carried off one of their sheep: and these who are governed by you are sheep. And why did you come hither? Was your desire in any danger? was your aversion ([Greek: echchlisis])? was your movement (pursuits)? was your avoidance of things? He replies, No; but the wife of my brother was carried off. Was it not then a great gain to be deprived of an adulterous wife? Shall we be despised then by the Trojans? What kind of people are the Trojans, wise or foolish? If they are wise, why do you fight with them? If they are fools, why do you care about them?

Do you possess the body then free or is it in servile condition? We do not know. Do you not know that it is the slave of fever, of gout, ophthalmia, dysentery, of a tyrant, of fire, of iron, of everything which is stronger? Yes, it is a slave. How then is it possible that anything which belongs to the body can be free from hindrance? and how is a thing great or valuable which is naturally dead, or earth, or mud? Well then, do you possess nothing which is free? Perhaps nothing. And who is able to compel you to assent to that which appears false? No man. And who can compel you not to assent to that which appears true? No man. By this then you see that there is something in you naturally free. But to desire or to be averse from, or to move towards an object or to move from it, or to prepare yourself, or to propose to do anything, which of you can do this, unless he has received an impression of the appearance of that which is profitable or a duty? No man. You have then in these things also something which is not hindered and is free. Wretched men, work out this, take care of this, seek for good here.

THAT WE OUGHT NOT TO BE MOVED BY A DESIRE OF THOSE THINGS WHICH ARE NOT IN OUR POWER.—Let not that which in another is contrary to nature be an evil to you; for you are not formed by nature to be depressed with others nor to be unhappy with others, but to be happy with them. If a man is unhappy, remember that his unhappiness is his own fault; for

God has made all men to be happy, to be free from perturbations. For this purpose he has given means to them, some things to each person as his own, and other things not as his own; some things subject to hindrance and compulsion and deprivation; and these things are not a man's own; but the things which are not subject to hindrances, are his own; and the nature of good and evil, as it was fit to be done by him who takes care of us and protects us like a father, he has made our own. But you say, I have parted from a certain person, and he is grieved. Why did he consider as his own that which belongs to another? why, when he looked on you and was rejoiced, did he not also reckon that you are a mortal, that it is natural for you to part from him for a foreign country? Therefore he suffers the consequences of his own folly. But why do you or for what purpose bewail yourself? Is it that you also have not thought of these things? but like poor women who are good for nothing, you have enjoyed all things in which you took pleasure, as if you would always enjoy them, both places and men and conversation; and now you sit and weep because you do not see the same persons and do not live in the same places. Indeed you deserve this, to be more wretched than crows and ravens who have the power of flying where they please and changing their nests for others, and crossing the seas without lamenting or regretting their former condition. Yes, but this happens to them because they are irrational creatures. Was reason then given to us by the gods for the purpose of unhappiness and misery, that we may pass our lives in wretchedness and lamentation? Must all persons be immortal and must no man go abroad, and must we ourselves not go abroad, but remain rooted like plants; and if any of our familiar friends goes abroad, must we sit and weep; and on the contrary, when he returns, must we dance and clap our hands like children?

But my mother laments when she does not see me. Why has she not learned these principles? and I do not say this, that we should not take care that she may not lament, but I say that we ought not to desire in every way what is not our own. And the sorrow of another is another's sorrow; but my sorrow is my own. I then will stop my own sorrow by every means, for it is in my power; and the sorrow of another I will endeavor to stop as far as I can; but I will not attempt to do it by every means; for if

I do, I shall be fighting against God, I shall be opposing Zeus and shall be placing myself against him in the administration of the universe; and the reward (the punishment) of this fighting against God and of this disobedience not only will the children of my children pay, but I also shall myself, both by day and by night, startled by dreams, perturbed, trembling at every piece of news, and having my tranquillity depending on the letters of others. Some person has arrived from Rome. I only hope there is no harm. But what harm can happen to you, where you are not? From Hellas (Greece) some one is come; I hope that there is no harm. In this way every place may be the cause of misfortune to you. Is it not enough for you to be unfortunate there where you are, and must you be so even beyond sea, and by the report of letters? Is this the way in which your affairs are in a state of security? Well then suppose that my friends have died in the places which are far from me. What else have they suffered than that which is the condition of mortals? Or how are you desirous at the same time to live to old age, and at the same time not to see the death of any person whom you love? Know you not that in the course of a long time many and various kinds of things must happen; that a fever shall overpower one, a robber another, and a third a tyrant? Such is the condition of things around us, such are those who live with us in the world; cold and heat, and unsuitable ways of living, and journeys by land, and voyages by sea, and winds, and various circumstances which surround us, destroy one man, and banish another, and throw one upon an embassy and another into an army. Sit down then in a flutter at all these things, lamenting, unhappy, unfortunate, dependent on another, and dependent not on one or two, but on ten thousands upon ten thousands.

Did you hear this when you were with the philosophers? did you learn this? do you not know that human life is a warfare? that one man must keep watch, another must go out as a spy, and a third must fight? and it is not possible that all should be in one place, nor is it better that it should be so. But you neglecting to do the commands of the general complain when anything more hard than usual is imposed on you, and you do not observe what you make the army become as far as it is in your power; that if all imitate you, no man will dig a trench, no man will put a rampart round, nor keep watch, nor expose himself to danger, but will appear to be useless for the purposes of an army. Again, in a vessel if you go as a sailor, keep to one place and stick to it. And if you are ordered to climb the mast, refuse; if to run to the head of the ship, refuse; and what master of a ship will endure you? and will he not pitch you overboard as a useless thing, an impediment only and bad example to the other sailors? And so it is here also: every man's life is a kind of warfare, and it is long and diversified. You must observe the duty of a soldier and do every thing at the nod of the general; if it is possible, divining what his wishes are; for there is no resemblance between that general and this, neither in strength nor in superiority of character. Know you not that a good man does nothing for the sake of appearance, but for the sake of doing right? What advantage is it then to him to have done right? And what advantage is it to a man who writes the name of Dion to write it as he ought? The advantage is to have written it. Is there no reward then? Do you seek a reward for a good man greater than doing what is good and just? At Olympia you wish for nothing more, but it seems to you enough to be crowned at the games. Does it seem to you so small and worthless a thing to be good and happy? For these purposes being introduced by the gods into this city (the world), and it being now your duty to undertake the work of a man, do you still want nurses also and a mamma, and do foolish women by their weeping move you and make you effeminate? Will you thus never cease to be a foolish child? know you not that he who does the acts of a child, the older he is, the more ridiculous he is?

So in this matter also: if you kiss your own child, or your brother or friend, never give full license to the appearance ([Greek: phantasian]), and allow not your pleasure to go as far as it chooses; but check it, and curb it as those who stand behind men in their triumphs and remind them that they are mortal. Do you also remind yourself in like manner, that he whom you love is mortal, and that what you love is nothing of your own; it has been given to you for the present, not that it should not be taken from you, nor has it been given to you for all time, but as a fig is given to you or a bunch of grapes at the appointed season of the year. But if you wish for these things in winter, you are a fool. So if you wish for your son or friend when it is not allowed to you, you must know that you are wishing for a fig in winter. For such as winter is to a fig, such is every event which happens from the universe to the things which are taken away according to its nature. And further, at the times when you are delighted with a thing, place before yourself the contrary appearances. What harm is it while you are kissing your child to say with a lisping voice: To-morrow you will die; and to a friend also: To-morrow you will go away or I shall, and never shall we see one another again? But these are words of bad omen—and some incantations also are of bad omen; but because they are useful, I don't care for this; only let them be useful. But do you call things to be of bad omen except those which are significant of some evil? Cowardice is a word of bad omen, and meanness of spirit, and sorrow, and grief, and shamelessness. These words are of bad omen; and yet we ought not to hesitate to utter them in order to protect ourselves against the things. Do you tell me that a name which is significant of any natural thing is of evil omen? say that even for the ears of corn to be reaped is of bad omen, for it signifies the destruction of the ears, but not of the world. Say that the falling of the leaves also is of bad omen, and for the dried fig to take the place of the green fig, and for raisins to be made from the grapes. For all these things are changes from a former state into other states; not a destruction, but a certain fixed economy and administration. Such is going away from home and a small change: such is death, a greater change, not from the state which now is to that which is not, but to that which is not now. Shall I then no longer exist? You will not exist, but you will be something else, of which the world now has need; for you also came into existence not when you chose, but when the world had need of you.

Let these thoughts be ready to hand by night and by day; these you should write, these you should read; about these you should talk to yourself and to others. Ask a man: Can you help me at all for this purpose? and further, go to another and to another. Then if anything that is said be contrary to your wish, this reflection first will immediately relieve you, that it is not unexpected. For it is a great thing in all cases to say: I knew that I begot a son who is mortal. For so you also will say: I knew that I am mortal, I knew that I may leave my home, I knew that I may be ejected from it, I knew that I may be led to prison. Then if you turn round and look to yourself, and seek the place from which comes that which has happened, you will forthwith recollect that it comes from the place of things which are out of the power of the will, and of things which are not my own. What then is it to me? Then, you will ask, and this is the chief thing: And who is it that sent it? The leader, or the general, the state, the law of the state. Give it me then, for I must always obey the law in everything. Then, when the appearance (of things) pains you, for it is not in your power to prevent this, contend against it by the aid of reason, conquer it: do not allow it to gain strength nor to lead you to the consequences by raising images such as it pleases and as it pleases. If you be in Gyara, do not imagine the mode of living at Rome, and how many pleasures there were for him who lived there and how many there would be for him who returned to Rome; but fix your mind on this matter, how a man who lives in Gyara ought to live in Gyara like a man of courage. And if you be in Rome, do not imagine what the life in Athens is, but think only of the life in Rome.

Then in the place of all other delights substitute this, that of being conscious that you are obeying God, that not in word, but in deed you are performing the acts of a wise and good man. For what a thing it is for a man to be able to say to himself: Now whatever the rest may say in solemn manner in the schools and may be judged to be saying in a way contrary to common opinion (or in a strange way), this I am doing; and they are sitting and are discoursing of my virtues and inquiring about me and praising me; and of this Zeus has willed that I shall receive from myself a demonstration, and shall myself know if he has a soldier such as he ought to have, a citizen such as he ought to have, and if he has chosen to produce me to the rest of mankind as a witness of the things which are independent of the will: See that you fear without reason, that you foolishly desire what you do desire; seek not the good in things external; seek it in yourselves: if you do not, you will not find it. For this purpose he leads me at one time hither, at another time sends me thither, shows me to men as poor, without authority, and sick; sends me to Gyara, leads me into prison, not because he hates me—far from him be such a meaning, for who hates the best of his servants? nor yet because he cares not for me, for he does not neglect any even of the smallest things; but he does this for the purpose of exercising me and making use of me as a witness to others. Being appointed to such a service, do I still care about the place in which I am, or with whom I am, or what men say about me? and do I not entirely direct my thoughts to God and to his instructions and commands?

Having these things (or thoughts) always in hand, and exercising them by yourself, and keeping them in readiness, you will never be in want of one to comfort you and strengthen you. For it is not shameful to be without something to eat, but not to have reason sufficient for keeping away fear and sorrow. But if once you have gained exemption from sorrow and fear, will there any longer be a tyrant for you, or a tyrant's guard, or attendants on Cæsar? Or shall any appointment to offices at court cause you pain, or shall those who sacrifice in the Capitol on the occasion of being named to certain functions, cause pain to you who have received so great authority from Zeus? Only do not make a proud display of it, nor boast of it; but show it by your acts; and if no man perceives it, be satisfied that you are yourself in a healthy state and happy.

TO THOSE WHO FALL OFF (DESIST) FROM THEIR PURPOSE.—Consider as to the things which you proposed to yourself at first, which you have secured, and which you have not; and how you are pleased when you recall to memory the one, and are pained about the other; and if it is possible, recover the things wherein you failed. For we must not shrink when we are engaged in the greatest combat, but we must even take blows. For the combat before us is not in wrestling and the Pancration, in which both the successful and the unsuccessful may have the greatest merit, or may have little, and in truth may be very fortunate or very unfortunate; but the combat is for good fortune and happiness themselves. Well then, even if we have renounced the contest in this matter (for good fortune and happiness), no man hinders us from renewing the combat again, and we are not compelled to wait for another four years that the games at Olympia may come again; but as soon as you have recovered and restored yourself, and employ the same zeal, you may renew the combat again; and if again you renounce it, you may again renew it; and if you once gain the victory, you are like him who has never renounced the combat. Only do not through a habit of doing the same thing (renouncing the combat), begin to do it with pleasure, and then like a bad athlete go about after being conquered in all the circuit of the games like quails who have run away.

TO THOSE WHO FEAR WANT.—Are you not ashamed at being more cowardly and more mean than fugitive slaves? How do they when they run away leave their masters? on what estates do they depend, and what domestics do they rely on? Do they not after stealing a little, which is enough for the first days, then afterwards move on through land or through sea, contriving one method after another for maintaining their lives? And what fugitive slave ever died of hunger? But you are afraid lest necessary things should fail you, and are sleepless by night. Wretch, are you so blind, and don't you see the road to which the want of necessaries leads?—Well, where does it lead?—to the same place to which a fever leads, or a stone that falls on you, to death. Have you not often said this yourself to your companions? have you not read much of this kind, and written much? and how often have you boasted that you were easy as to death?

Learn then first what are the things which are shameful, and then tell us that you are a philosopher: but at present do not, even if any other man calls you so, allow it.

Is that shameful to you which is not your own act, that of which you are not the cause, that which has come to you by accident, as a headache, as a fever? If your parents were poor, and left their property to others, and if while they live, they do not help you at all, is this shameful to you? Is this what you learned with the philosophers? Did you never hear that the thing which is shameful ought to be blamed, and that which is blamable is worthy of blame? Whom do you blame for an act which is not his own, which he did not do himself? Did you then make your father such as he is, or is it in your power to improve him? Is this power given to you? Well then, ought you to wish the things which are not given to you, or to be ashamed if you do not obtain them? And have you also been accustomed while you were studying philosophy to look to others and to hope for nothing from yourself? Lament then and groan and eat with fear that you may not have food to-morrow. Tremble about your poor slaves lest they steal, lest they run away, lest they die. So live, and continue to live, you who in name only have approached philosophy, and have disgraced its theorems as far as you can by showing them to be useless and unprofitable to those who take them up; you, who have never sought constancy, freedom from perturbation, and from passions; you who have not sought any person for the sake of this object, but many for the sake of syllogisms; you who have never thoroughly examined any of these appearances by yourself, Am I able to bear, or am I not able to bear? What remains for me to do? But as if all your affairs were well and secure, you have been resting on the third topic, that of things being unchanged, in order that you may possess unchanged—what? cowardice, mean spirit, the admiration of the rich, desire without attaining any end, and avoidance ([Greek: echchlisin]) which fails in the attempt? About security in these things you have been anxious.

Ought you not to have gained something in addition from reason, and then to have protected this with security? And whom did you ever see building a battlement all around and encircling it with a wall? And what doorkeeper is placed with no door to watch? But you practise in order to be able to prove—what? You practise that you may not be tossed as on the sea through sophisms, and tossed about from what? Show me first what you hold, what you measure, or what you weigh; and show me the scales or the medimnus (the measure); or how long will you go on measuring the dust? Ought you not to demonstrate those things which make men happy, which make things go on for them in the way as they wish, and why we ought to blame no man, accuse no man, and acquiesce in the administration of the universe?

ABOUT FREEDOM.—He is free who lives as he wishes to live; who is neither subject to compulsion nor to hindrance, nor to force; whose movements to action ([Greek: hormai]) are not impeded, whose desires attain their purpose, and who does not fall into that which he would avoid ([Greek: echchliseis aperiptotoi]). Who then chooses to live in error? No man. Who chooses to live deceived, liable to mistake, unjust, unrestrained, discontented, mean? No man. Not one then of the bad lives as he wishes; nor is he then free. And who chooses to live in sorrow, fear, envy, pity, desiring and failing in his desires, attempting to avoid something and falling into it? Not one. Do we then find any of the bad free from sorrow, free from fear, who does not fall into that which he would avoid, and does not obtain that which he wishes? Not one; nor then do we find any bad man free.

Further, then, answer me this question, also: does freedom seem to you to be something great and noble and valuable? How should it not seem so? Is it possible then when a man obtains anything so great and valuable and noble to be mean? It is not possible. When then you see any man subject to another or flattering him contrary to his own opinion, confidently affirm that this man also is not free; and not only if he do this for a bit of supper, but also if he does it for a government (province) or a consulship; and call these men little slaves who for the sake of little matters do these things, and those who do so for the sake of great things call great slaves, as they deserve to be. This is admitted also. Do you think that freedom is a thing independent and self-governing? Certainly. Whomsoever then it is in the power of another to hinder and compel, declare that he is not free. And do not look, I entreat you, after his grandfathers and great-grandfathers, or inquire about his being bought or sold, but if you hear him saying from his heart and with feeling, "Master," even if the twelve fasces precede him (as consul), call him a slave. And if you hear him say, "Wretch that I am, how much I suffer," call him a slave. If, finally, you see him lamenting, complaining, unhappy, call him a slave, though he wears a praetexta. If, then, he is doing nothing of this kind do not yet say that he is free, but learn his opinions, whether they are subject to compulsion, or may produce hindrance, or to bad fortune, and if you find him such, call him a slave who has a holiday in the Saturnalia; say that his master is from home; he will return soon, and you will know what he suffers.

What then is that which makes a man free from hindrance

and makes him his own master? For wealth does not do it, nor consulship, nor provincial government, nor royal power; but something else must be discovered. What then is that which when we write makes us free from hindrance and unimpeded? The knowledge of the art of writing. What then is it in playing the lute? The science of playing the lute. Therefore in life also it is the science of life. You have then heard in a general way; but examine the thing also in the several parts. Is it possible that he who desires any of the things which depend on others can be free from hindrance? No. Is it possible for him to be unimpeded? No. Therefore he cannot be free. Consider then, whether we have nothing which is in our own power only, or whether we have all things, or whether some things are in our own power, and others in the power of others. What do you mean? When you wish the body to be entire (sound) is it in your power or not? It is not in my power. When you wish it to be healthy? Neither is this in my power. When you wish it to be handsome? Nor is this. Life or death? Neither is this in my power. Your body then is another's, subject to every man who is stronger than yourself. It is. But your estate is it in your power to have it when you please, and as long as you please, and such as you please? No. And your slaves? No. And your clothes? No. And your house? No. And your horses? Not one of these things. And if you wish by all means your children to live, or your wife, or your brother, or your friends, is it in your power? This also is not in my power.

Whether then have you nothing which is in your own power, which depends on yourself only and cannot be taken from you, or have you anything of the kind? I know not. Look at the thing then thus, and examine it. Is any man able to make you assent to that which is false? No man. In the matter of assent then you are free from hindrance and obstruction. Granted. Well; and can a man force you to desire to move towards that to which you do not choose? He can, for when he threatens me with death or bonds he compels me to desire to move towards it. If then you despise death and bonds, do you still pay any regard to him? No. Is then the despising of death an act of your own or is it not yours? It is my act.

When you have made this preparation, and have practised

this discipline, to distinguish that which belongs to another from that which is your own, the things which are subject to hindrance from those which are not, to consider the things free from hindrance to concern yourself, and those which are not free not to concern yourself, to keep your desire steadily fixed to the things which do concern yourself, and turned from the things which do not concern yourself; do you still fear any man? No one. For about what will you be afraid? About the things which are your own, in which consists the nature of good and evil? and who has power over these things? who can take them away? who can impede them? No man can, no more than he can impede God. But will you be afraid about your body and your possessions, about things which are not yours, about things which in no way concern you? and what else have you been studying from the beginning than to distinguish between your own and not your own, the things which are in your power and not in your power, the things subject to hindrance and not subject? and why have you come to the philosophers? was it that you may nevertheless be unfortunate and unhappy? You will then in this way, as I have supposed you to have done, be without fear and disturbance. And what is grief to you? for fear comes from what you expect, but grief from that which is present. But what further will you desire? For of the things which are within the power of the will, as being good and present, you have a proper and regulated desire; but of the things which are not in the power of the will you do not desire any one, and so you do not allow any place to that which is irrational, and impatient, and above measure hasty.

Then after receiving everything from another and even yourself, are you angry and do you blame the giver if he takes anything from you? Who are you, and for what purpose did you come into the world? Did not he (God) introduce you here, did he not show you the light, did he not give you fellow-workers, and perceptions and reason? and as whom did he introduce you here? did he not introduce you as subject to death, and as one to live on the earth with a little flesh, and to observe his administration, and to join with him in the spectacle and the festival for a short time? Will you not then, as long as you have been permitted, after seeing the spectacle and the solemnity, when he leads you out, go with adoration of him and thanks for what you have heard and seen? No; but I would still enjoy the feast. The initiated too would wish to be longer in the initiation; and perhaps also those at Olympia to see other athletes. But the solemnity is ended; go away like a grateful and modest man; make room for others; others also must be born, as you were, and, being born, they must have a place, and houses, and necessary things. And if the first do not retire, what remains? Why are you insatiable? Why are you not content? why do you contract the world? Yes, but I would have my little children with me and my wife. What, are they yours? do they not belong to the giver, and to him who made you? then will you not give up what belongs to others? will you not give way to him who is superior? Why then did he introduce me into the world on these conditions? And if the conditions do not suit you, depart. He has no need of a spectator who is not satisfied. He wants those who join in the festival, those who take part in the chorus, that they may rather applaud, admire, and celebrate with hymns the solemnity. But those who can bear no trouble, and the cowardly, he will not unwillingly see absent from the great assembly ([Greek: panaeguris]) for they did not when they were present behave as they ought to do at a festival nor fill up their place properly, but they lamented, found fault with the deity, fortune, their companions; not seeing both what they had, and their own powers, which they received for contrary purposes, the powers of magnanimity, of a generous mind, manly spirit, and what we are now inquiring about, freedom. For what purpose then have I received these things? To use them. How long? So long as he who has lent them chooses. What if they are necessary to me? Do not attach yourself to them and they will not be necessary; do not say to yourself that they are necessary, and then they are not necessary.

You then, a man may say, are you free? I wish, by the gods, and pray to be free; but I am not yet able to face my masters, I still value my poor body, I value greatly the preservation of it entire, though I do not possess it entire. But I can point out to you a free man, that you may no longer seek an example. Diogenes was free. How was he free? Not because he was born of free parents, but because he was himself free, because he had cast off all the handles of slavery, and it was not possible for any man to approach him, nor had any man the means of laying hold of him to enslave him. He had everything easily loosed, everything only hanging to him. If you laid hold of his property, he would have rather let it go and be yours, than he would have followed you for it; if you had laid hold of his leg, he would have let go his leg; if of all his body, all his poor body; his intimates, friends, country, just the same. For he knew from whence he had them, and from whom, and on what conditions. His true parents indeed, the gods, and his real country he would never have deserted, nor would he have yielded to any man in obedience to them and to their orders, nor would any man have died for his country more readily. For he was not used to inquire when he should be considered to have done anything on behalf of the whole of things (the universe, or all the world), but he remembered that everything which is done comes from thence and is done on behalf of that country and is commanded by him who administers it. Therefore see what Diogenes himself says and writes: "For this reason," he says, "Diogenes, it is in your power to speak both with the King of the Persians and with Archidamus the King of the Lacedaemonians, as you please." Was it because he was born of free parents? I suppose all the Athenians and all the Lacedaemonians, because they were born of slaves, could not talk with them (these kings) as they wished, but feared and paid court to them. Why then does he say that it is in his power? Because I do not consider the poor body to be my own, because I want nothing, because law is everything to me, and nothing else is. These were the things which permitted him to be free.

Think of these things, these opinions, these words; look to these examples, if you would be free, if you desire the thing according to its worth. And what is the wonder if you buy so great a thing at the price of things so many and so great? For the sake of this which is called liberty, some hang themselves, others throw themselves down precipices, and sometimes even whole cities have perished; and will you not for the sake of the true and unassailable and secure liberty give back to God when he demands them the things which he has given? Will you not, as Plato says, study not to die only, but also to endure torture, and exile, and scourging, and, in a word, to give up all which is not your own? If you will not, you will be a slave among slaves, even if you be ten thousand times a consul; and if you make your way up to the palace (Cæsar's residence), you will no less be a slave; and you will feel that perhaps philosophers utter words which are contrary to common opinion (paradoxes), as Cleanthes also said, but not words contrary to reason. For you will know by experience that the words are true, and that there is no profit from the things which are valued and eagerly sought to those who have obtained them; and to those who have not yet obtained them there is an imagination ([Greek: phantasia]), that when these things are come, all that is good will come with them; then, when they are come, the feverish feeling is the same, the tossing to and fro is the same, the satiety, the desire of things, which are not present; for freedom is acquired not by the full possession of the things which are desired, but by removing the desire. And that you may know that this is true, as you have labored for those things, so transfer your labor to these: be vigilant for the purpose of acquiring an opinion which will make you free; pay court to a philosopher instead of to a rich old man; be seen about a philosopher's doors; you will not disgrace yourself by being seen; you will not go away empty nor without profit, if you go to the philosopher as you ought, and if not (if you do not succeed), try at least; the trial (attempt) is not disgraceful.

ON FAMILIAR INTIMACY.—To this matter before all you must attend, that you be never so closely connected with any of your former intimates or friends as to come down to the same acts as he does. If you do not observe this rule, you will ruin yourself. But if the thought arises in your mind, "I shall seem disobliging to him and he will not have the same feeling towards me," remember that nothing is done without cost, nor is it possible for a man if he does not do the same things to be the same man that he was. Choose then which of the two you will have, to be equally loved by those by whom you were formerly loved, being the same with your former self; or, being superior, not to obtain from your friends the same that you did before.

WHAT THINGS WE SHOULD EXCHANGE FOR OTHER THINGS.—Keep this thought in readiness, when you lose anything external, what you acquire in place of it; and if it be worth more, never say, I have had a loss; neither if you have got a horse in place of an ass, or an ox in place of a sheep, nor a good action in place of a bit of money, nor in place of idle talk such tranquillity as befits a man, nor in place of lewd talk if you have acquired modesty. If you remember this, you will always maintain your character such as it ought to be. But if you do not, consider that the times of opportunity are perishing, and that whatever pains you take about yourself, you are going to waste them all and overturn them. And it needs only a few things for the loss and overturning of all—namely, a small deviation from reason. For the steerer of a ship to upset it, he has no need of the same means as he has need of for saving it; but if he turns it a little to the wind, it is lost; and if he does not do this purposely, but has been neglecting his duty a little, the ship is lost. Something of the kind happens in this case also; if you only fall a nodding a little, all that you have up to this time collected is gone. Attend therefore to the appearances of things, and watch over them; for that which you have to preserve is no small matter, but it is modesty and fidelity and constancy, freedom from the affects, a state of mind undisturbed, freedom from fear, tranquillity, in a word liberty. For what will you sell these things? See what is the value of the things which you will obtain in exchange for these.— But shall I not obtain any such thing for it?—See, and if you do in return get that, see what you receive in place of it. I possess decency, he possesses a tribuneship: he possesses a prætorship, I possess modesty. But I do not make acclamations where it is not becoming: I will not stand up where I ought not; for I am free, and a friend of God. and so I obey him willingly. But I must not claim (seek) anything else, neither body nor possession, nor magistracy, nor good report, nor in fact anything. For he (God) does not allow me to claim (seek) them, for if he had chosen, he would have made them good for me; but he has not done so, and for this reason I cannot transgress his commands. Preserve that which is your own good in everything; and as to every other thing, as it is permitted, and so far as to behave consistently with reason in respect to them, content with this only. If you do not, you will be unfortunate, you will fail in all things, you will be hindered, you will be impeded. These are the laws which have been sent from thence (from God); these are the orders. Of these laws a man ought to be an expositor, to these he ought to submit, not to those of Masurius and Cassius.

TO THOSE WHO ARE DESIROUS OF PASSING LIFE IN TRANQUILLITY.—Remember that not only the desire of power and of riches makes us mean and subject to others, but even the desire of tranquillity, and of leisure, and of travelling abroad, and of learning. For, to speak plainly, whatever the external thing may be, the value which we set upon it places us in subjection to others. What then is the difference between desiring to be a senator or not desiring to be one; what is the difference between desiring power or being content with a private station; what is the difference between saying, I am unhappy, I have nothing to do, but I am bound to my books as a corpse; or saying, I am unhappy, I have no leisure for reading? For as salutations and power are things external and independent of the will, so is a book. For what purpose do you choose to read? Tell me. For if you only direct your purpose to being amused or learning something, you are a silly fellow and incapable of enduring labor. But if you refer reading to the proper end, what else is this than a tranquil and happy life ([Greek: eusoia])? But if reading does not secure for you a happy and tranquil life, what is the use of it? But it does secure this, the man replies, and for this reason I am vexed that I am deprived of it.—And what is this tranquil and happy life, which any man can impede, I do not say Cæsar or Cæsar's friend, but a crow, a piper, a fever, and thirty thousand other things? But a tranquil and happy life contains nothing so sure as continuity and freedom from obstacle. Now I am called to do something: I will go then with the purpose of observing the measures (rules) which I must keep, of acting with modesty, steadiness, without desire and aversion to things external; and then that I may attend to men, what they say, how they are moved; and this not with any bad disposition, or that I may have something to blame or to ridicule; but I turn to myself, and ask if I also commit the same faults. How then shall I cease to commit them? Formerly I also acted wrong, but now I do not: thanks to God.

What then is the reason of this? The reason is that we have never read for this purpose, we have never written for this purpose, so that we may in our actions use in a way conformable to nature the appearances presented to us; but we terminate in this, in learning what is said, and in being able to expound it to another, in resolving a syllogism, and in handling the hypothetical syllogism. For this reason where our study (purpose) is, there alone is the impediment. Would you have by all means the things which are not in your power? Be prevented then, be hindered, fail in your purpose. But if we read what is written about action (efforts, [Greek: hormae]), not that we may see what is said about action, but that we may act well; if we read what is said about desire and aversion (avoiding things), in order that we may neither fail in our desires, nor fall into that which we try to avoid; if we read what is said about duty (officium), in order that remembering the relations (of things to one another) we may do nothing irrationally nor contrary to these relations; we should not be vexed, in being hindered as to our readings, but we should be satisfied with doing the acts which are conformable (to the relations), and we should be reckoning not what so far we have been accustomed to reckon: To-day I have read so many verses, I have written so many; but (we should say), To-day I have employed my action as it is taught by the philosophers; I have not employed my desire; I have used avoidance ([Greek: echchlisei]) only with respect to things which are within the power of my will; I have not been afraid of such a person, I have not been prevailed upon by the entreaties of another; I have exercised my patience, my abstinence, my co-operation with others; and so we should thank God for what we ought to thank him.

There is only one way to happiness, and let this rule be ready both in the morning and during the day and by night: the rule is not to look towards things which are out of the power of our will, to think that nothing is our own, to give up all things to the Divinity, to Fortune; to make them the superintendents of these things, whom Zeus also has made so; for a man to observe that only which is his own, that which cannot be hindered; and when we read, to refer our reading to this only, and our writing and our listening. For this reason I cannot call the man industrious, if I hear this only, that he reads and writes; and even if a man adds that he reads all night, I cannot say so, if he knows not to what he should refer his reading. For neither do you say that a man is industrious if he keeps awake for a girl, nor do I. But if he does it (reads and writes) for reputation, I say that he is a lover of reputation. And if he does it for money, I say that he is a lover of money, not a lover of labor; and if he does it through love of learning, I say that he is a lover of learning. But if he refers his labor to his own ruling power that he may keep it in a state conformable to nature and pass his life in that state, then only do I say that he is industrious. For never commend a man on account of these things which are common to all, but on account of his opinions (principles); for these are the things which belong to each man, which make his actions bad or good. Remembering these rules, rejoice in that which is present, and be content with the things which come in season. If you see anything which you have learned and inquired about occurring to you in your course of life (or opportunely applied by you to the acts of life), be delighted at it. If you have laid aside or have lessened bad disposition and a habit of reviling; if you have done so with rash temper, obscene words, hastiness, sluggishness; if you are not moved by what you formerly were, and not in the same way as you once were, you can celebrate a festival daily, to-day because you have behaved well in one act, and to-morrow because you have behaved well in another. How much greater is this a reason for making sacrifices than a consulship or the government of a province? These things come to you from yourself and from the gods. Remember this, who gives these things and to whom, and for what purpose. If you cherish yourself in these thoughts, do you still think that it makes any difference where you shall be happy, where you shall please God? Are not the gods equally distant from all places? Do they not see from all places alike that which is going on?

AGAINST THE QUARRELSOME AND FEROCIOUS.—The wise and good man neither himself fights with any person, nor does he allow another, so far as he can prevent it. And an example of this as well as of all other things is proposed to us in the life of Socrates, who not only himself on all occasions avoided fights (quarrels), but would not allow even others to quarrel. See in Xenophon's Symposium how many quarrels he settled, how further he endured Thrasymachus and Polus and Callicles; how he tolerated his wife, and how he tolerated his son who attempted to confute him and to cavil with him. For he remembered well that no man has in his power another man's ruling principle. He wished therefore for nothing else than that which was his own. And what is this? Not that this or that man may act according to nature, for that is a thing which belongs to another; but that while others are doing their own acts, as they choose, he may nevertheless be in a condition conformable to nature and live in it, only doing what is his own to the end that others also may be in a state conformable to nature. For this is the object always set before him by the wise and good man. Is it to be commander (a prætor) of an army? No; but if it is permitted him, his object is in this matter to maintain his own ruling principle. Is it to marry? No; but if marriage is allowed to him, in this matter his object is to maintain himself in a condition conformable to nature. But if he would have his son not to do wrong or his wife, he would have what belongs to another not to belong to another: and to be instructed is this, to learn what things are a man's own and what belongs to another.

How then is there left any place for fighting (quarrelling) to a man who has this opinion (which he ought to have)? Is he surprised at any thing which happens, and does it appear new to him? Does he not expect that which comes from the bad to be worse and more grievous than that what actually befalls him? And does he not reckon as pure gain whatever they (the bad) may do which falls short of extreme wickedness? Such a person has reviled you. Great thanks to him for not having struck you. But he has struck me also. Great thanks that he did not wound you. But he wounded me also. Great thanks that he did not kill you. For when did he learn or in what school that man is a tame animal, that men love one another, that an act of injustice is a great harm to him who does it. Since then he has not learned this and is not convinced of it, why shall he not follow that which seems to be for his own interest? Your neighbor has thrown stones. Have you then done anything wrong? But the things in the house have been broken. Are you then a utensil? No; but a free power of will. What then is given to you (to do) in answer to this? If you are like a wolf, you must bite in return, and throw more stones. But, if you consider what is proper for a man, examine your storehouse, see with what faculties you came into the world. Have you the disposition of a wild beast, have you the disposition of revenge for an injury? When is a horse wretched? When he is deprived of his natural faculties, not when he cannot crow like a cock, but when he cannot run. When is a dog wretched? Not when he cannot fly, but when he cannot track his game. Is then a man also unhappy in this way, not because he cannot strangle lions or embrace statues, for he did not come into the world in the possession of certain powers from nature for this purpose, but because he has lost his probity and his fidelity? People ought to meet and lament such a man for the misfortunes into which he has fallen; not indeed to lament because a man has been born or has died, but because it has happened to him in his lifetime to have lost the things which are his own, not that which he received from his father, not his land and house, and his inn, and his slaves; for not one of these things is a man's own, but all belong to others, are servile, and subject to account ([Greek: hupeithuna]), at different times given to different persons by those who have them in their power: but I mean the things which belong to him as a man, the marks (stamps) in his mind with which he came into the world, such as we seek also on coins, and if we find them we approve of the coins, and if we do not find the marks we reject them. What is the stamp on this sestertius? The stamp of Trajan. Present it. It is the stamp of Nero. Throw it away; it cannot be accepted, it is counterfeit. So also in this case: What is the stamp of his opinions? It is gentleness, a sociable disposition, a tolerant temper, a disposition to mutual affections. Produce these qualities. I accept them: I consider this man a citizen, I accept him as a neighbor, a companion in my voyages. Only see that he has not Nero's stamp. Is he passionate, is he full of resentment, is he fault-finding? If the whim seizes him, does he break the heads of those who come in his way? (If so), why then did you say that he is a man? Is everything judged (determined) by the bare form? If that is so, say that the form in wax is an apple and has the smell and the taste of an apple. But the external figure is not enough: neither then is the nose enough and the eyes to make the man, but he must have the opinions of a man. Here is a man who does not listen to reason, who does not know when he is refuted: he is an ass; in another man the sense of shame is become dead: he is good for nothing, he is anything rather than a man. This man seeks whom he may meet and kick or bite, so that he is not even a sheep or an ass, but a kind of wild beast.

What then? would you have me to be despised?—By whom? by those who know you? and how shall those who know you despise a man who is gentle and modest? Perhaps you mean by those who do not know you? What is that to you? For no other artisan cares for the opinion of those who know not his art. But they will be more hostile to me for this reason. Why do you say "me"? Can any man injure your will, or prevent you from using in a natural way the appearances which are presented to you? In no way can he. Why then are you still disturbed and why do you choose to show yourself afraid? And why do you not come forth and proclaim that you are at peace with all men whatever they may do, and laugh at those chiefly who think that they can harm you? These slaves, you can say, know not either who I am, nor where lies my good or my evil, because they have no access to the things which are mine.

In this way also those who occupy a strong city mock the besiegers (and say): What trouble these men are now taking for nothing; our wall is secure, we have food for a very long time, and all other resources. These are the things which make a city strong and impregnable; but nothing else than his opinions makes a man's soul impregnable. For what wall is so strong, or what body is so hard, or what possession is so safe, or what honor (rank, character) so free from assault (as a man's opinions)? All (other) things everywhere are perishable, easily taken by assault, and if any man in any way is attached to them, he must be disturbed, except what is bad, he must fear, lament, find his desires disappointed, and fall into things which he would avoid. Then do we not choose to make secure the only means of safety which are offered to us, and do we not choose to withdraw ourselves from that which is perishable and servile and to labor at the things which are imperishable and by nature free; and do we not remember that no man either hurts another or does good to another, but that a man's opinions about each thing, is that which hurts him, is that which overturns him; this is fighting, this is civil discord, this is war? That which made Eteocles and Polynices enemies was nothing else than this opinion which they had about royal power, their opinion about exile, that the one is the extreme of evils, the other the greatest good. Now this is the nature of every man to seek the good, to avoid the bad; to consider him who deprives us of the one and involves us in the other an enemy and treacherous, even if he be a brother, or a son, or a father. For nothing is more akin to us than the good; therefore, if these things (externals) are good and evil, neither is a father a friend to sons, nor a brother to a brother, but all the world is everywhere full of enemies, treacherous men, and sycophants. But if the will ([Greek: proairesis], the purpose, the intention) being what it ought to be, is the only good; and if the will being such as it ought not to be, is the only evil, where is there any strife, where is there reviling? about what? about the things which do not concern us? and strife with whom? with the ignorant, the unhappy, with those who are deceived about the chief things?

Remembering this Socrates managed his own house and endured a very ill-tempered wife and a foolish (ungrateful?) son.

AGAINST THOSE WHO LAMENT OVER BEING PITIED.—I am grieved, a man says, at being pitied. Whether then is the fact of your being pitied a thing which concerns you or those who pity you? Well, is it in your power to stop this pity? It is in my power, if I show them that I do not require pity. And whether then are you in the condition of not deserving (requiring) pity, or are you not in that condition? I think that I am not; but these persons do not pity me, for the things for which, if they ought to pity me, it would be proper, I mean, for my faults; but they pity me for my poverty, for not possessing honorable offices, for diseases and deaths and other such things. Whether then are you prepared to convince the many, that not one of these things is an evil, but that it is possible for a man who is poor and has no office ([Greek: anarchonti]) and enjoys no honor to be happy; or to show yourself to them as rich and in power? For the second of these things belong to a man who is boastful, silly, and good for nothing. And consider by what means the pretence must be supported. It will be necessary for you to hire slaves and to possess a few silver vessels, and to exhibit them in public, if it is possible, though they are often the same, and to attempt to conceal the fact that they are the same, and to have splendid garments, and all other things for display, and to show that you are a man honored by the great, and to try to sup at their houses, or to be supposed to sup there, and as to your person to employ some mean arts, that you may appear to be more handsome and nobler than you are. These things you must contrive, if you choose to go by the second path in order not to be pitied. But the first way is both impracticable and long, to attempt the very thing which Zeus has not been able to do, to convince all men what things are good and bad. Is this power given to you? This only is given to you, to convince yourself; and you have not convinced yourself. Then I ask you, do you attempt to persuade other men? and who has lived so long with you as you with yourself? and who has so much power of convincing you as you have of convincing yourself; and who is better disposed and nearer to you than you are to yourself? How then have you not yet convinced yourself in order to learn? At present are not things upside down? Is this what you have been earnest about doing, to learn to be free from grief and free from disturbance, and not to be humbled (abject), and to be free? Have you not heard then that there is only one way which leads to this end, to give up (dismiss) the things which do not depend on the will, to withdraw from them, and to admit that they belong to others? For another man then to have an opinion about you, of what kind is it? It is a thing independent of the will—Then is it nothing to you? It is nothing. When then you are still vexed at this and disturbed, do you think that you are convinced about good and evil?

ON FREEDOM FROM FEAR.—What makes the tyrant formidable? The guards, you say, and their swords, and the men of the bedchamber, and those who exclude them who would enter. Why then if you bring a boy (child) to the tyrant when he is with his guards, is he not afraid; or is it because the child does not understand these things? If then any man does understand what guards are and that they have swords, and comes to the tyrant for this very purpose because he wishes to die on account of some circumstance and seeks to die easily by the hand of another, is he afraid of the guards? No, for he wishes for the thing which makes the guards formidable. If then any man neither wishing to die nor to live by all means, but only as it may be permitted, approaches the tyrant what hinders him from approaching the tyrant without fear? Nothing. If then a man has the same opinion about his property as the man whom I have instanced has about his body; and also about his children and his wife, and in a word is so affected by some madness or despair that he cares not whether he possesses them or not, but like children who are playing with shells (quarrel) about the play, but do not trouble themselves about the shells, so he too has set no value on the materials (things), but values the pleasure that he has with them and the occupation, what tyrant is then formidable to him, or what guards or what swords?

What hinders a man, who has clearly separated (comprehended) these things, from living with a light heart and bearing easily the reins, quietly expecting everything which can happen, and enduring that which has already happened? Would you have me to bear poverty? Come and you will know what poverty is when it has found one who can act well the part of a poor man. Would you have me to possess power? Let me have power, and also the trouble of it. Well, banishment? Wherever I shall go, there it will be well with me; for here also where I am, it was not because of the place that it was well with me, but because of my opinions which I shall carry off with me, for neither can any man deprive me of them; but my opinions alone are mine and they cannot be taken from me, and I am satisfied while I have them, wherever I may be and whatever I am doing. But now it is time to die. Why do you say to die? Make no tragedy show of the thing, but speak of it as it is. It is now time for the matter (of the body) to be resolved into the things out of which it was composed. And what is the formidable thing here? what is going to perish of the things which are in the universe? what new thing or wondrous is going to happen? Is it for this reason that a tyrant is formidable? Is it for this reason that the guards appear to have swords which are large and sharp? Say this to others; but I have considered about all these things; no man has power over me. I have been made free; I know his commands, no man can now lead me as a slave. I have a proper person to assert my freedom; I have proper judges. (I say) are you not the master of my body? What then is that to me? Are you not the master of my property? What then is that to me? Are you not the master of my exile or of my chains? Well, from all these things and all the poor body itself I depart at your bidding, when you please. Make trial of your power, and you will know how far it reaches.

Whom then can I still fear? Those who are over the bedchamber? Lest they should do, what? Shut me out? If they find that I wish to enter, let them shut me out. Why then do you go to the doors? Because I think it befits me, while the play (sport) lasts, to join in it. How then are you not shut out? Because unless some one allows me to go in, I do not choose to go in, but am always content with that which happens; for I think that what God chooses is better than what I choose. I will attach myself as a minister and follower to him; I have the same movements (pursuits) as he has, I have the same desires; in a word, I have the same will ([Greek: sunthelo]). There is no shutting out for me, but for those who would force their way in. Why then do not I force my way in? Because I know that nothing good is distributed within to those who enter. But when I hear any man called fortunate because he is honored by Cæsar, I say what does he happen to get? A province (the government of a province). Does he also obtain an opinion such as he ought? The office of a Prefect. Does he also obtain the power of using his office well? Why do I still strive to enter (Cæsar's chamber)? A man scatters dried figs and nuts: the children seize them, and fight with one another; men do not, for they think them to be a small matter. But if a man should throw about shells, even the children do not seize them. Provinces are distributed: let children look to that. Money is distributed; let children look to that. Prætorships, consulships, are distributed; let children scramble for them, let them be shut out, beaten, kiss the hands of the giver, of the slaves: but to me these are only dried figs and nuts. What then? If you fail to get them, while Cæsar is scattering them about, do not be troubled; if a dried fig come into your lap, take it and eat it; for so far you may value even a fig. But if I shall stoop down and turn another over, or be turned over by another, and shall flatter those who have got into (Cæsar's) chamber, neither is a dried fig worth the trouble, nor anything else of the things which are not good, which the philosophers have persuaded me not to think good.

TO A PERSON WHO HAD BEEN CHANGED TO A CHARACTER OF SHAMELESSNESS.—When you see another man in the possession of power (magistracy), set against this the fact that you have not the want (desire) of power; when you see another rich, see what you possess in place of riches: for if you possess nothing in place of them, you are miserable; but if you have not the want of riches, know that you possess more than this man possesses and what is worth much more.

WHAT THINGS WE OUGHT TO DESPISE AND WHAT THINGS WE OUGHT TO VALUE.—The difficulties of all men are about external things, their helplessness is about external. What shall I do? how will it be? how will it turn out? will this happen? will that? All these are the words of those who are turning themselves to things which are not within the power of the will. For who says, How shall I not assent to that which is false? how shall I not turn away from the truth? If a man be of such a good disposition as to be anxious about these things I will remind him of this: Why are you anxious? The thing is in your own power, be assured; do not be precipitate in assenting before you apply the natural rule. On the other side, if a man is anxious (uneasy) about desire, lest it fail in its purpose and miss its end, and with respect to the avoidance of things, lest he should fall into that which he would avoid, I will first kiss (love) him, because he throws away the things about which others are in a flutter (others desire) and their fears, and employs his thoughts about his own affairs and his own condition. Then I shall say to him: If you do not choose to desire that which you will fail to obtain nor to attempt to avoid that into which you will fall, desire nothing which belongs to (which is in the power of) others, nor try to avoid any of the things which are not in your power. If you do not observe this rule, you must of necessity fail in your desires and fall into that which you would avoid. What is the difficulty here? where is there room for the words How will it be? and How will it turn out? and Will this happen or that?

Now is not that which will happen independent of the will? Yes. And the nature of good and of evil, is it not in the things which are within the power of the will? Yes. Is it in your power then to treat according to nature everything which happens? Can any person hinder you? No man. No longer then say to me, How will it be? For, however it may be, you will dispose of it well, and the result to you will be a fortunate one. What would Hercules have been if he said: How shall a great lion not appear to me, or a great boar, or savage men? And what do you care for that? If a great boar appear, you will fight a greater fight; if bad men appear, you will relieve the earth of the bad. Suppose then that I lose my life in this way. You will die a good man, doing a noble act. For since he must certainly die, of necessity a man must be found doing something, either following the employment of a husbandman, or digging, or trading, or serving in a consulship, or suffering from indigestion or from diarrhoea. What then do you wish to be doing when you are found by death? I, for my part, would wish to be found doing something which belongs to a man, beneficent, suitable to the general interest, noble. But if I cannot be found doing things so great, I would be found doing at least that which I cannot be hindered from doing, that which is permitted me to do, correcting myself, cultivating the faculty which makes use of appearances, laboring at freedom from the affects (laboring at tranquillity of mind); rendering to the relations of life their due. If I succeed so far, also (I would be found) touching on (advancing to) the third topic (or head) safety in forming judgments about things. If death surprises me when I am busy about these things, it is enough for me if I can stretch out my hands to God and say: The means which I have received from thee for seeing thy administration (of the world) and following it I have not neglected; I have not dishonored thee by my acts; see how I have used my perceptions, see how I have used my preconceptions; have I ever blamed thee? have I been discontented with anything that happens, or wished it to be otherwise? have I wished to transgress the (established) relations (of things)? That thou hast given me life, I thank thee for what thou hast given. So long as I have used the things which are thine I am content. Take them back and place them wherever thou mayest choose, for thine were all things, thou gavest them to me. Is it not enough to depart in this state of mind? and what life is better and more becoming than that of a man who is in this state of mind? and what end is more happy?

ABOUT PURITY (CLEANLINESS).—Some persons raise a question whether the social feeling is contained in the nature of man; and yet I think that these same persons would have no doubt that love of purity is certainly contained in it, and that if man is distinguished from other animals by anything, he is distinguished by this. When then we see any other animal cleaning itself, we are accustomed to speak of the act with surprise, and to add that the animal is acting like a man; and on the other hand, if a man blames an animal for being dirty, straightway, as if we were making an excuse for it, we say that of course the animal is not a human creature. So we suppose that there is something superior in man, and that we first receive it from the gods. For since the gods by their nature are pure and free from corruption, so far as men approach them by reason, so far do they cling to purity and to a love (habit) of purity. But since it is impossible that man's nature ([Greek: ousia]) can be altogether pure, being mixed (composed) of such materials, reason is applied, as far as it is possible, and reason endeavors to make human nature love purity.

The first then and highest purity is that which is in the soul; and we say the same of impurity. Now you could not discover the impurity of the soul as you could discover that of the body; but as to the soul, what else could you find in it than that which makes it filthy in respect to the acts which are her own? Now the acts of the soul are movement towards an object or movement from it, desire, aversion, preparation, design (purpose), assent. What then is it which in these acts makes the soul filthy and impure? Nothing else than her own bad judgments ([Greek: chrimata]). Consequently the impurity of the soul is the soul's bad opinions; and the purification of the soul is the planting in it of proper opinions; and the soul is pure which has proper opinions, for the soul alone in her own acts is free from perturbation and pollution.

For we ought not even by the appearance of the body to deter the multitude from philosophy; but as in other things, a philosopher should show himself cheerful and tranquil, so also he should in the things that relate to the body. See, ye men, that I have nothing, that I want nothing; see how I am without a house, and without a city, and an exile, if it happens to be so, and without a hearth I live more free from trouble and more happily than all of noble birth and than the rich. But look at my poor body also and observe that it is not injured by my hard way of living. But if a man says this to me, who has the appearance (dress) and face of a condemned man, what god shall persuade me to approach philosophy, if it makes men such persons? Far from it; I would not choose to do so, even if I were going to become a wise man. I indeed would rather that a young man, who is making his first movements towards philosophy, should come to me with his hair carefully trimmed than with it dirty and rough, for there is seen in him a certain notion (appearance) of beauty and a desire of (attempt at) that which is becoming; and where he supposes it to be, there also he strives that it shall be. It is only necessary to show him (what it is), and to say: Young man, you seek beauty, and you do well; you must know then that it (is produced) grows in that part of you where you have the rational faculty; seek it there where you have the movements towards and movements from things, where you have the desires towards and the aversion from things; for this is what you have in yourself of a superior kind; but the poor body is naturally only earth; why do you labor about it to no purpose? if you shall learn nothing else, you will learn from time that the body is nothing. But if a man comes to me daubed with filth, dirty, with a moustache down to his knees, what can I say to him, by what kind of resemblance can I lead him on? For about what has he busied himself which resembles beauty, that I may be able to change him and say, Beauty is not in this, but in that? Would you have me to tell him, that beauty consists not in being daubed with muck, but that it lies in the rational part? Has he any desire of beauty? has he any form of it in his mind? Go and talk to a hog, and tell him not to roll in the mud.

ON ATTENTION.—When you have remitted your attention for a short time, do not imagine this, that you will recover it when you choose; but let this thought be present to you, that in consequence of the fault committed today your affairs must be in a worse condition for all that follows. For first, and what causes most trouble, a habit of not attending is formed in you; then a habit of deferring your attention. And continually from time to time you drive away by deferring it the happiness of life, proper behavior, the being and living conformably to nature. If then the procrastination of attention is profitable, the complete omission of attention is more profitable; but if it is not profitable, why do you not maintain your attention constant? Today I choose to play. Well then, ought you not to play with attention? I choose to sing. What then hinders you from doing so with attention? Is there any part of life excepted, to which attention does not extend? For will you do it (anything in life) worse by using attention, and better by not attending at all? And what else of the things in life is done better by those who do not use attention? Does he who works in wood work better by not attending to it? Does the captain of a ship manage it better by not attending? and are any of the smaller acts done better by inattention? Do you not see that when you have let your mind loose, it is no longer in your power to recall it, either to propriety, or to modesty, or to moderation; but you do everything that comes into your mind in obedience to your inclinations.

First then we ought to have these (rules) in readiness, and to do nothing without them, and we ought to keep the soul directed to this mark, to pursue nothing external, and nothing which belongs to others (or is in the power of others), but to do as he has appointed who has the power; we ought to pursue altogether the things which are in the power of the will, and all other things as it is permitted. Next to this we ought to remember who we are, and what is our name, and to endeavor to direct our duties towards the character (nature) of our several relations (in life) in this manner: what is the season for singing, what is the season for play, and in whose presence; what will be the consequence of the act; whether our associates will despise us, whether we shall despise them; when to jeer ([Greek: schopsai]), and whom to ridicule; and on what occasion to comply and with whom; and finally, in complying how to maintain our own character. But wherever you have deviated from any of these rules, there is damage immediately, not from anything external, but from the action itself.

What then? is it possible to be free from faults (if you do all this)? It is not possible; but this is possible, to direct your efforts incessantly to being faultless. For we must be content if by never remitting this attention we shall escape at least a few errors. But now when you have said, Tomorrow I will begin to attend, you must be told that you are saying this, Today I will be shameless, disregardful of time and place, mean; it will be in the power of others to give me pain; today I will be passionate and envious. See how many evil things you are permitting yourself to do. If it is good to use attention tomorrow, how much better is it to do so today? if tomorrow it is in your interest to attend, much more is it today, that you may be able to do so tomorrow also, and may not defer it again to the third day.

AGAINST OR TO THOSE WHO READILY TELL THEIR OWN AFFAIRS.—When a man has seemed to us to have talked with simplicity (candor) about his own affairs, how is it that at last we are ourselves also induced to discover to him our own secrets and we think this to be candid behavior? In the first place, because it seems unfair for a man to have listened to the affairs of his neighbor, and not to communicate to him also in turn our own affairs; next, because we think that we shall not present to them the appearance of candid men when we are silent about our own affairs. Indeed, men are often accustomed to say, I have told you all my affairs, will you tell me nothing of your own? where is this done? Besides, we have also this opinion that we can safely trust him who has already told us his own affairs; for the notion rises in our mind that this man could never divulge our affairs because he would be cautious that we also should not divulge his. In this way also the incautious are caught by the soldiers at Rome. A soldier sits by you in a common dress and begins to speak ill of Cæsar; then you, as if you had received a pledge of his fidelity by his having begun the abuse, utter yourself also what you think, and then you are carried off in chains.

Something of this kind happens to us also generally. Now as this man has confidently intrusted his affairs to me, shall I also do so to any man whom I meet? (No), for when I have heard, I keep silence, if I am of such a disposition; but he goes forth and tells all men what he has heard. Then, if I hear what has been done, if I be a man like him, I resolve to be revenged, I divulge what he has told me; I both disturb others, and am disturbed myself. But if I remember that one man does not injure another, and that every man's acts injure and profit him, I secure this, that I do not anything like him, but still I suffer what I do suffer through my own silly talk.

True, but it is unfair when you have heard the secrets of your neighbor for you in your turn to communicate nothing to him. Did I ask you for your secrets, my man? did you communicate your affairs on certain terms, that you should in return hear mine also? If you are a babbler and think that all who meet you are friends, do you wish me also to be like you? But why, if you did well in intrusting your affairs to me, and it is not well for me to intrust mine to you, do you wish me to be so rash? It is just the same as if I had a cask which is water-tight, and you one with a hole in it, and you should come and deposit with me your wine that I might put it into my cask, and then should complain that I also did not intrust my wine to you, for you have a cask with a hole in it. How then is there any equality here? You intrusted your affairs to a man who is faithful and modest, to a man who thinks that his own actions alone are injurious and (or) useful, and that nothing external is. Would you have me intrust mine to you, a man who has dishonored his own faculty of will, and who wishes to gain some small bit of money or some office or promotion in the court (emperor's palace), even if you should be going to murder your own children, like Medea? Where (in what) is this equality (fairness)? But show yourself to me to be faithful, modest, and steady; show me that you have friendly opinions; show that your cask has no hole in it; and you will see how I shall not wait for you to trust me with your own affairs, but I myself shall come to you and ask you to hear mine. For who does not choose to make use of a good vessel? Who does not value a benevolent and faithful adviser? Who will not willingly receive a man who is ready to bear a share, as we may say, of the difficulty of his circumstances, and by this very act to ease the burden, by taking a part of it.

THE GOLDEN SAYINGS

I

Are these the only works of Providence within us? What words suffice to praise or set them forth? Had we but understanding, should we ever cease hymning and blessing the Divine Power, both openly and in secret, and telling of His gracious gifts? Whether digging or ploughing or eating, should we not sing the hymn to God:—

Great is God, for that He hath given us such instruments to till the ground withal: Great is God, for that He hath given us hands and the power of swallowing and digesting; of unconsciously growing and breathing while we sleep!

Thus should we ever have sung; yea and this, the grandest and divinest hymn of all:—

Great is God, for that He hath given us a mind to apprehend these things, and duly to use them!

What then! seeing that most of you are blinded, should there not be some one to fill this place, and sing the hymn to God on behalf of all men? What else can I that am old and lame do but sing to God? Were I a nightingale, I should do after the manner of a nightingale. Were I a swan, I should do after the manner of a swan. But now, since I am a reasonable being, I must sing to God: that is my work: I do it, nor will I desert this my post, as long as it is granted me to hold it; and upon you too I call to join in this self-same hymn.

II

How then do men act? As though one returning to his

country who had sojourned for the night in a fair inn, should be so captivated thereby as to take up his abode there.

"Friend, thou hast forgotten thine intention! This was not thy destination, but only lay on the way thither."

"Nay, but it is a proper place."

"And how many more of the sort there may be; only to pass through upon thy way! Thy purpose was to return to thy country; to relieve thy kinsmen's fears for thee; thyself to discharge the duties of a citizen; to marry a wife, to beget offspring, and to fill the appointed round of office. Thou didst not come to choose out what places are most pleasant; but rather to return to that wherein thou wast born and where wert appointed to be a citizen."

III

Try to enjoy the great festival of life with other men.

IV

But I have one whom I must please, to whom I must be subject, whom I must obey:—God, and those who come next to Him. He hath entrusted me with myself: He hath made my will subject to myself alone and given me rules for the right use thereof.

V

Rufus used to say, If you have leisure to praise me, what I say is naught. In truth he spoke in such wise, that each of us who sat there, though that some one had accused him to Rufus:—so surely did he lay his finger on the very deeds we did: so surely display the faults of each before his very eyes.

VI

But what saith God?—"Had it been possible, Epictetus, I would have made both that body of thine and thy possessions free and unimpeded, but as it is, be not deceived:—it is not thine own; it is but finely tempered clay. Since then this I could not do, I have given thee a portion of Myself, in the power of desiring and declining and of pursuing and avoiding, and in a word the power of dealing with the things of sense. And if thou neglect not this, but place all that thou hast therein, thou shalt never be let or hindered; thou shalt never lament; thou shalt not blame or flatter any. What then? Seemth this to thee a little thing?"—God forbid!—"Be content then therewith!"

And so I pray the Gods.

VII

What saith Antisthenes? Hast thou never heard?— It is a kingly thing, O Cyrus, to do well and to be evil spoken of.

VIII

"Aye, but to debase myself thus were unworthy of me."

"That," said Epictetus, "is for you to consider, not for me. You know yourself what you are worth in your own eyes; and at what price you will sell yourself. For men sell themselves at various prices. This was why, when Florus was deliberating whether he should appear at Nero's shows, taking part in the performance himself, Agrippinus replied, 'But why do not you appear?' he answered, 'Because I do not even consider the question.' For the man who has once stooped to consider such questions, and to reckon up the value of external things, is not far from forgetting what manner of man he is. Why, what is it that you ask me? Is death preferable, or life? I reply, Life. Pain or pleasure? I reply, Pleasure."

"Well, but if I do not act, I shall lose my head."

"Then go and act! But for my part I will not act."

"Why?"

"Because you think yourself but one among the many threads which make up the texture of the doublet. You should aim at being like men in general—just as your thread has no ambition either to be anything distinguished compared with the other threads. But I desire to be the purple—that small and shining part which makes the rest seem fair and beautiful. Why then do you bid me become even as the multitude? Then were I no longer the purple."

IX

If a man could be throughly penetrated, as he ought, with this thought, that we are all in an especial manner sprung from God, and that God is the Father of men as well as of Gods, full surely he would never conceive aught ignoble or base of himself. Whereas if Cæsar were to adopt you, your haughty looks would be intolerable; will you not be elated at knowing that you are the son of God? Now however it is not so with us: but seeing that in our birth these two things are commingled—the body which we share with the animals, and the Reason and Thought which we share with the Gods, many decline towards this unhappy kinship with the dead, few rise to the blessed kinship with the Divine. Since then every one must deal with each thing according to the view which he forms about it, those few who hold that they are born for fidelity, modesty, and unerring sureness in dealing with the things of sense, never conceive aught base or ignoble of themselves: but the multitude the contrary. Why, what am I?—A wretched human creature; with this miserable flesh of mine. Miserable indeed! but you have something better than that paltry flesh of yours. Why then cling to the one, and neglect the other?

X

Thou art but a poor soul laden with a lifeless body.

XI

The other day I had an iron lamp placed beside my household gods. I heard a noise at the door and on hastening down found my lamp carried off. I reflected that the culprit was in no very strange case. "Tomorrow, my friend," I said, "you will find an earthenware lamp; for a man can only lose what he has."

XII

The reason why I lost my lamp was that the thief was superior to me in vigilance. He paid however this price for the lamp, that in exchange for it he consented to become a thief: in exchange for it, to become faithless.

XIII

But God hath introduced Man to be a spectator of Himself

and of His works; and not a spectator only, but also an interpreter of them. Wherefore it is a shame for man to begin and to leave off where the brutes do. Rather he should begin there, and leave off where Nature leaves off in us: and that is at contemplation, and understanding, and a manner of life that is in harmony with herself.

See then that ye die not without being spectators of these things.

XIV

You journey to Olympia to see the work of Phidias; and each of you holds it a misfortune not to have beheld these things before you die. Whereas when there is no need even to take a journey, but you are on the spot, with the works before you, have you no care to contemplate and study these?

Will you not then perceive either who you are or unto what end you were born: or for what purpose the power of contemplation has been bestowed on you?

"Well, but in life there are some things disagreeable and hard to bear."

And are there none at Olympia? Are you not scorched by the heat? Are you not cramped for room? Have you not to bathe with discomfort? Are you not drenched when it rains? Have you not to endure the clamor and shouting and such annoyances as these? Well, I suppose you set all this over against the splendour of the spectacle and bear it patiently. What then? have you not received greatness of heart, received courage, received fortitude? What care I, if I am great of heart, for aught that can come to pass? What shall cast me down or disturb me? What shall seem painful? Shall I not use the power to the end for which I received it, instead of moaning and wailing over what comes to pass?

XV

If what philosophers say of the kinship of God and Man be true, what remains for men to do but as Socrates did:—never, when asked one's country, to answer, "I am an Athenian or a Corinthian," but "I am a citizen of the world."

XVI

He that hath grasped the administration of the World, who hath learned that this Community, which consists of God and men, is the foremost and mightiest and most comprehensive of all:—that from God have descended the germs of life, not to my father only and father's father, but to all things that are born and grow upon the earth, and in an especial manner to those endowed with Reason (for those only are by their nature fitted to hold communion with God, being by means of Reason conjoined with Him)—why should not such an one call himself a citizen of the world? Why not a son of God? Why should he fear aught that comes to pass among men? Shall kinship with Cæsar, or any other of the great at Rome, be enough to hedge men around with safety and consideration, without a thought of apprehension: while to have God for our Maker, and Father, and Kinsman, shall not this set us free from sorrows and fears?

XVII

I do not think that an old fellow like me need have been sitting here to try and prevent your entertaining abject notions of yourselves, and talking of yourselves in an abject and ignoble way: but to prevent there being by chance among you any such young men as, after recognising their kindred to the Gods, and their bondage in these chains of the body and its manifold necessities, should desire to cast them off as burdens too grievous to be borne, and depart their true kindred. This is the struggle in which your Master and Teacher, were he worthy of the name, should be engaged. You would come to me and say: "Epictetus, we can no longer endure being chained to this wretched body, giving food and drink and rest and purification: aye, and for its sake forced to be subservient to this man and that. Are these not things indifferent and nothing to us? Is it not true that death is no evil? Are we not in a manner kinsmen of the Gods, and have we not come from them? Let us depart thither, whence we came: let us be freed from these chains that confine and press us down. Here are thieves and robbers and tribunals: and they that are called tyrants, who deem that they have after a fashion power over us, because of the miserable body and what appertains to it. Let us show them that they have power over none."

XVIII

And to this I reply:—
"Friends, wait for God. When He gives the signal, and releases you from this service, then depart to Him. But for the present, endure to dwell in the place wherein He hath assigned you your post. Short indeed is the time of your habitation therein, and easy to those that are minded. What tyrant, what robber, what tribunals have any terrors for those who thus esteem the body and all that belong to it as of no account? Stay; depart not rashly hence!"

XIX

Something like that is what should pass between a teacher and ingenuous youths. As it is, what does pass? The teacher is a lifeless body, and you are lifeless bodies yourselves. When you have had enough to eat today, you sit down and weep about tomorrow's food. Slave! if you have it, well and good; if not, you will depart: the door is open—why lament? What further room is there for tears? What further occasion for flattery? Why should one envy another? Why should you stand in awe of them that have much or are placed in power, especially if they be also strong and passionate? Why, what should they do to us? What they can do, we will not regard: what does concern us, that they cannot do. Who then shall rule one that is thus minded?

XX

Seeing this then, and noting well the faculties which you have, you should say,—"Send now, O God, any trial that Thou wilt; lo, I have means and powers given me by Thee to acquit myself with honour through whatever comes to pass!"—No; but there you sit, trembling for fear certain things should come to pass, and moaning and groaning and lamenting over what does come to pass. And then you upbraid the Gods. Such meanness of spirit can have but one result—impiety.

Yet God has not only given us these faculties by means of which we may bear everything that comes to pass without being crushed or depressed thereby; but like a good King and Father, He has given us this without let or hindrance, placed wholly at our own disposition, without reserving to Himself any power of impediment or restraint. Though possessing all these things free and all you own, you do not use them! you do not perceive what it is you have received nor whence it comes, but sit moaning and groaning; some of you blind to the Giver, making no acknowledgment to your Benefactor; others basely giving themselves to complaints and accusations against God.

Yet what faculties and powers you possess for attaining courage and greatness of heart, I can easily show you; what you have for upbraiding and accusation, it is for you to show me!

XXI

How did Socrates bear himself in this regard? How else than as became one who was fully assured that he was the kinsman of Gods?

XXII

If God had made that part of His own nature which He severed from Himself and gave to us, liable to be hindered or constrained either by Himself or any other, He would not have been God, nor would He have been taking care of us as He ought . . . . If you choose, you are free; if you choose, you need blame no man—accuse no man. All things will be at once according to your mind and according to the Mind of God.

XXIII

Petrifaction is of two sorts. There is petrifaction of the understanding; and also of the sense of shame. This happens when a man obstinately refuses to acknowledge plain truths, and persists in maintaining what is self-contradictory. Most of us dread mortification of the body, and would spare no pains to escape anything of that kind. But of mortification of the soul we are utterly heedless. With regard, indeed, to the soul, if a man is in such a state as to be incapable of following or understanding anything, I grant you we do think him in a bad way. But mortification of the sense of shame and modesty we go so far as to dub strength of mind!

XXIV

If we were as intent upon our business as the old fellows

at Rome are upon what interests them, we too might perhaps accomplish something. I know a man older than I am, now Superintendent of the Corn-market at Rome, and I remember when he passed through this place on his way back from exile, what an account he gave me of his former life, declaring that for the future, once home again, his only care should be to pass his remaining years in quiet and tranquility. "For how few years have I left!" he cried. "That," I said, "you will not do; but the moment the scent of Rome is in your nostrils, you will forget it all; and if you can but gain admission to Court, you will be glad enough to elbow your way in, and thank God for it." "Epictetus," he replied, "if ever you find me setting as much as one foot within the Court, think what you will of me."

Well, as it was, what did he do? Ere ever he entered the city, he was met by a despatch from the Emperor. He took it, and forgot the whole of his resolutions. From that moment, he has been piling one thing upon another. I should like to be beside him to remind him of what he said when passing this way, and to add, How much better a prophet I am than you!

What then? do I say man is not made for an active life? Far from it! . . . But there is a great difference between other men's occupations and ours. . . . A glance at theirs will make it clear to you. All day long they do nothing but calculate, contrive, consult how to wring their profit out of food-stuffs, farm-plots and the like. . . . Whereas, I entreat you to learn what the administration of the World is, and what place a Being endowed with reason holds therein: to consider what you are yourself, and wherein your Good and Evil consists.

XXV

A man asked me to write to Rome on his behalf who, as most people thought, had met with misfortune; for having been before wealthy and distinguished, he had afterwards lost all and was living here. So I wrote about him in a humble style. He however on reading the letter returned it to me, with the words: "I asked for your help, not for your pity. No evil has happened unto me."

XXVI

True instruction is this:—to learn to wish that each thing should come to pass as it does. And how does it come to pass? As the Disposer has disposed it. Now He has disposed that there should be summer and winter, and plenty and dearth, and vice and virtue, and all such opposites, for the harmony of the whole.

XXVII

Have this thought ever present with thee, when thou losest any outward thing, what thou gainest in its stead; and if this be the more precious, say not, I have suffered loss.

XXVIII

Concerning the Gods, there are who deny the very existence of the Godhead; others say that it exists, but neither bestirs nor concerns itself nor has forethought for anything. A third party attribute to it existence and forethought, but only for great and heavenly matters, not for anything that is on earth. A fourth party admit things on earth as well as in heaven, but only in general, and not with respect to each individual. A fifth, of whom were Ulysses and Socrates are those that cry:—
I move not without Thy knowledge!

XXIX

Considering all these things, the good and true man submits his judgement to Him that administers the Universe, even as good citizens to the law of the State. And he that is being instructed should come thus minded:—How may I in all things follow the Gods; and, How may I rest satisfied with the Divine Administration; and, How may I become free? For he is free for whom all things come to pass according to his will, and whom none can hinder. What then, is freedom madness? God forbid. For madness and freedom exist not together.

"But I wish all that I desire to come to pass and in the manner that I desire."

—You are mad, you are beside yourself. Know you not that Freedom is a glorious thing and of great worth? But that what I desired at random I should wish at random to come to pass, so far from being noble, may well be exceeding base.

XXX

You must know that it is no easy thing for a principle to become a man's own, unless each day he maintain it and hear it maintained, as well as work it out in life.

XXXI

You are impatient and hard to please. If alone, you call it solitude: if in the company of men, you dub them conspirators and thieves, and find fault with your very parents, children, brothers, and neighbours. Whereas when by yourself you should have called it Tranquillity and Freedom: and herein deemed yourself like unto the Gods. And when in the company of many, you should not have called it a wearisome crowd and tumult, but an assembly and a tribunal; and thus accepted all with contentment.

XXXII

What then is the chastisement of those who accept it not? To be as they are. Is any discontented with being alone? let him be in solitude. Is any discontented with his parents? let him be a bad son, and lament. Is any discontented with his children? let him be a bad father.—"Throw him into prison!"—What prison?—Where he is already: for he is there against his will; and wherever a man is against his will, that to him is a prison. Thus Socrates was not in prison, since he was there with his own consent.

XXXIII

Knowest thou what a speck thou art in comparison with the Universe?—-That is, with respect to the body; since with respect to Reason, thou art not inferior to the Gods, nor less than they. For the greatness of Reason is not measured by length or height, but by the resolves of the mind. Place then thy happiness in that wherein thou art equal to the Gods.

XXXIV

Asked how a man might eat acceptably to the Gods, Epictetus replied:—If when he eats, he can be just, cheerful, equable, temperate, and orderly, can he not thus eat acceptably to the Gods? But when you call for warm water, and your slave does not answer, or when he answers brings it lukewarm, or is not even found to be in the house at all, then not to be vexed nor burst with anger, is not that acceptable to the Gods?

"But how can one endure such people?"

Slave, will you not endure your own brother, that has God to his forefather, even as a son sprung from the same stock, and of the same high descent as yourself? And if you are stationed in a high position, are you therefor forthwith set up for a tyrant? Remember who you are, and whom you rule, that they are by nature your kinsmen, your brothers, the offspring of God.

"But I paid a price for them, not they for me."

Do you see whither you are looking—down to the earth, to the pit, to those despicable laws of the dead? But to the laws of the Gods you do not look.

XXXV

When we are invited to a banquet, we take what is set before us; and were one to call upon his host to set fish upon the table or sweet things, he would be deemed absurd. Yet in a word, we ask the Gods for what they do not give; and that, although they have given us so many things!

XXXVI

Asked how a man might convince himself that every single act of his was under the eye of God, Epictetus answered:—

"Do you not hold that things on earth and things in heaven are continuous and in unison with each other?"

"I do," was the reply.

"Else how should the trees so regularly, as though by God's command, at His bidding flower; at His bidding send forth shoots, bear fruit and ripen it; at His bidding let it fall and shed their leaves, and folded up upon themselves lie in quietness and rest? How else, as the Moon waxes and wanes, as the Sun approaches and recedes, can it be that such vicissitude and alternation is seen in earthly things?

"If then all things that grow, nay, our own bodies, are thus bound up with the whole, is not this still truer of our souls? And if our souls are bound up and in contact with God, as being very parts and fragments plucked from Himself, shall He not feel every movement of theirs as though it were His own, and belonging to His own nature?"

XXXVII

"But," you say, "I cannot comprehend all this at once."
"Why, who told you that your powers were equal to God's?"
Yet God hath placed by the side of each a man's own Guardian Spirit, who is charged to watch over him—a Guardian who sleeps not nor is deceived. For to what better or more watchful Guardian could He have committed which of us? So when you have shut the doors and made a darkness within, remember never to say that you are alone; for you are not alone, but God is within, and your Guardian Spirit, and what light do they need to behold what you do? To this God you also should have sworn allegiance, even as soldiers unto Cæsar. They, when their service is hired, swear to hold the life of Cæsar dearer than all else: and will you not swear your oath, that are deemed worthy of so many and great gifts? And will you not keep your oath when you have sworn it? And what oath will you swear? Never to disobey, never to arraign or murmur at aught that comes to you from His hand: never unwillingly to do or suffer aught that necessity lays upon you.
"Is this oath like theirs?"
They swear to hold no other dearer than Cæsar: you, to hold our true selves dearer than all else beside.

XXXVIII

"How shall my brother cease to be wroth with me?"
Bring him to me, and I will tell him. But to thee I have

nothing to say about his anger.

XXXIX

When one took counsel of Epictetus, saying, "What I seek is this, how even though my brother be not reconciled to me, I may still remain as Nature would have me to be," he replied: "All great things are slow of growth; nay, this is true even of a grape or of a fig. If then you say to me now, I desire a fig, I shall answer, It needs time: wait till it first flower, then cast its blossom, then ripen. Whereas then the fruit of the fig-tree reaches not maturity suddenly nor yet in a single hour, do you nevertheless desire so quickly, and easily to reap the fruit of the mind of man?—Nay, expect it not, even though I bade you!"

XL

Epaphroditus had a shoemaker whom he sold as being good-for-nothing. This fellow, by some accident, was afterwards purchased by one of Cæsar's men, and became a shoemaker to Cæsar. You should have seen what respect Epaphroditus paid him then. "How does the good Felicion? Kindly let me know!" And if any of us inquired, "What is Epaphroditus doing?" the answer was, "He is consulting about so and so with Felicion."— Had he not sold him as good-for-nothing? Who had in a trice converted him into a wiseacre?

This is what comes of holding of importance anything but the things that depend on the Will.

XLI

What you shun enduring yourself, attempt not to impose on others. You shun slavery—beware of enslaving others! If you can endure to do that, one would think you had been once upon a time a slave yourself. For Vice has nothing in common with virtue, nor Freedom with slavery.

XLII

Has a man been raised to tribuneship? Every one that he meets congratulates him. One kisses him on the eyes, another on the neck, while the slaves kiss his hands. He goes home to find torches burning; he ascends to the Capitol to sacrifice.— Who ever sacrificed for having had right desires; for having conceived such inclinations as Nature would have him? In truth we thank the Gods for that wherein we place our happiness.

XLIII

A man was talking to me to-day about the priesthood of Augustus. I said to him, "Let the thing go, my good Sir; you will spend a good deal to no purpose."

"Well, but my name will be inserted in all documents and contracts."

"Will you be standing there to tell those that read them, That is my name written there? And even if you could now be there in every case, what will you do when you are dead?"

"At all events my name will remain."

"Inscribe it on a stone and it will remain just as well. And think, beyond Nicopolis what memory of you will there be?"

"But I shall have a golden wreath to wear."

"If you must have a wreath, get a wreath of roses and put it on; you will look more elegant!"

XLIV

Above all, remember that the door stands open. Be not more fearful than children; but as they, when they weary of the game, cry, "I will play no more," even so, when thou art in the like case, cry, "I will play no more" and depart. But if thou stayest, make no lamentation.

XLV

Is there smoke in the room? If it be slight, I remain; if grievous, I quit it. For you must remember this and hold it fast, that the door stands open.
"You shall not dwell at Nicopolis!"
Well and good.
"Nor at Athens."
Then I will not dwell at Athens either.
"Nor at Rome."
Nor at Rome either.
"You shall dwell in Gyara!"
Well: but to dwell in Gyara seems to me like a grievous smoke; I depart to a place where none can forbid me to dwell: that habitation is open unto all! As for the last garment of all, that is the poor body; beyond that, none can do aught unto me. This why Demetrius said to Nero: "You threaten me with death; it is Nature who threatens you!"

XLVI

The beginning of philosophy is to know the condition of one's own mind. If a man recognises that this is in a weakly state, he will not then want to apply it to questions of the greatest moment. As it is, men who are not fit to swallow even a morsel, buy whole treatises and try to devour them. Accordingly they either vomit them up again, or suffer from indigestion, whence come gripings, fluxions, and fevers. Whereas they should have stopped to consider their capacity.

XLVII

In theory it is easy to convince an ignorant person: in actual life, men not only object to offer themselves to be convinced, but hate the man who has convinced them. Whereas Socrates used to say that we should never lead a life not subjected to examination.

XLVIII

This is the reason why Socrates, when reminded that he should prepare for his trial, answered: "Thinkest thou not that I have been preparing for it all my life?"
"In what way?"
"I have maintained that which in me lay!"
"How so?"
"I have never, secretly or openly, done a wrong unto any."

XLIX

In what character dost thou now come forward?
As a witness summoned by God. "Come thou," saith God, "and testify for me, for thou art worthy of being brought forward as a witness by Me. Is aught that is outside thy will either good or bad? Do I hurt any man? Have I placed the good of each

in the power of any other than himself? What witness dost thou bear to God?"

"I am in evil state, Master, I am undone! None careth for me, none giveth me aught: all men blame, all speak evil of me."

Is this the witness thou wilt bear, and do dishonour to the calling wherewith He hath called thee, because He hath done thee so great honour, and deemed thee worthy of being summoned to bear witness in so great a cause?

L

Wouldst thou have men speak good of thee? speak good of them. And when thou hast learned to speak good of them, try to do good unto them, and thus thou wilt reap in return their speaking good of thee.

LI

When thou goest in to any of the great, remember that Another from above sees what is passing, and that thou shouldst please Him rather than man. He therefore asks thee:—

"In the Schools, what didst thou call exile, imprisonment, bonds, death and shame?"

"I called them things indifferent."

"What then dost thou call them now? Are they at all changed?"

"No."

"Is it then thou that art changed?"

"No."

"Say then, what are things indifferent?"

"Things that are not in our power."

"Say then, what follows?"

"That things which are not in our power are nothing to me."

"Say also what things you hold to be good."

"A will such as it ought to be, and a right use of the things of sense."

"And what is the end?"

"To follow Thee!"

LII

"That Socrates should ever have been so treated by the Athenians!"

Slave! why say "Socrates"? Speak of the thing as it is: That ever then the poor body of Socrates should have been dragged away and haled by main force to prison! That ever hemlock should have been given to the body of Socrates; that that should have breathed its life away!—Do you marvel at this? Do you hold this unjust? Is it for this that you accuse God? Had Socrates no compensation for this? Where then for him was the ideal Good? Whom shall we hearken to, you or him? And what says he?

"Anytus and Melitus may put me to death: to injure me is beyond their power."

And again:—

"If such be the will of God, so let it be."

LIII

Nay, young man, for heaven's sake; but once thou hast heard these words, go home and say to thyself:—"It is not Epictetus that has told me these things: how indeed should he? No, it is some gracious God through him. Else it would never have entered his head to tell me them—he that is not used to speak to any one thus. Well, then, let us not lie under the wrath of God, but be obedient unto Him."—-Nay, indeed; but if a raven by its croaking bears thee any sign, it is not the raven but God that sends the sign through the raven; and if He signifies anything to thee through human voice, will He not cause the man to say these words to thee, that thou mayest know the power of the

Divine—how He sends a sign to some in one way and to others in another, and on the greatest and highest matters of all signifies His will through the noblest messenger?

What else does the poet mean:—

> I spake unto him erst Myself, and sent
> Hermes the shining One, to check and warn him,
> The husband not to slay, nor woo the wife!

LIV

In the same way my friend Heraclitus, who had a trifling suit about a petty farm at Rhodes, first showed the judges that his cause was just, and then at the finish cried, "I will not entreat you: nor do I care what sentence you pass. It is you who are on your trial, not I!"—And so he ended the case.

LV

As for us, we behave like a herd of deer. When they flee from the huntsman's feathers in affright, which way do they turn? What haven of safety do they make for? Why, they rush upon the nets! And thus they perish by confounding what they should fear with that wherein no danger lies. . . . Not death or pain is to be feared, but the fear of death or pain. Well said the poet therefore:—

Death has no terror; only a Death of shame!

LVI

How is it then that certain external things are said to be natural, and other contrary to Nature?

Why, just as it might be said if we stood alone and apart from others. A foot, for instance, I will allow it is natural should be clean. But if you take it as a foot, and as a thing which does not stand by itself, it will beseem it (if need be) to walk in the mud, to tread on thorns, and sometimes even to be cut off, for the benefit of the whole body; else it is no longer a foot. In some such way we should conceive of ourselves also. What art thou?—A man.— Looked at as standing by thyself and separate, it is natural for thee in health and wealth long to live. But looked at as a Man, and only as a part of a Whole, it is for that Whole's sake that thou shouldest at one time fall sick, at another brave the perils of the sea, again, know the meaning of want and perhaps die an early death. Why then repine? Knowest thou not that as the foot is no more a foot if detached from the body, so thou in like case art no longer a Man? For what is a Man? A part of a City:—first of the City of Gods and Men; next, of that which ranks nearest it, a miniature of the universal City. . . . In such a body, in such a world enveloping us, among lives like these, such things must happen to one or another. Thy part, then, being here, is to speak of these things as is meet, and to order them as befits the matter.

LVII

That was a good reply which Diogenes made to a man who asked him for letters of recommendation.—"That you are a man, he will know when he sees you;—whether a good or bad one, he will know if he has any skill in discerning the good or bad. But if he has none, he will never know, though I write him a thousand times."—It is as though a piece of silver money desired to be recommended to some one to be tested. If the man be a good judge of silver, he will know: the coin will tell its own tale.

LVIII

Even as the traveller asks his way of him that he meets, inclined in no wise to bear to the right rather than to the left (for he desires only the way leading whither he would go), so should we come unto God as to a guide; even as we use our eyes without admonishing them to show us some things rather than others, but content to receive the images of such things as they present to us. But as it is we stand anxiously watching the victim, and with the voice of supplication call upon the augur:—"Master, have mercy on me: vouchsafe unto me a way of escape!" Slave, would you then have aught else then what is best? is there anything better than what is God's good pleasure? Why, as far as in you lies, would you corrupt your Judge, and lead your Counsellor astray?

LIX

God is beneficent. But the Good also is beneficent. It should seem then that where the real nature of God is, there too is to be found the real nature of the Good. What then is the real nature of God?—Intelligence, Knowledge, Right Reason. Here then without more ado seek the real nature of the Good. For surely thou dost not seek it in a plant or in an animal that reasoneth not.

LX

Seek then the real nature of the Good in that without whose presence thou wilt not admit the Good to exist in aught else.— What then? Are not these other things also works of God?—They are; but not preferred to honour, nor are they portions of God. But thou art a thing preferred to honour: thou art thyself a fragment torn from God:—thou hast a portion of Him within thyself. How is it then that thou dost not know thy high descent—dost not know whence thou comest? When thou eatest, wilt thou not remember who thou art that eatest and whom thou feedest? In intercourse, in exercise, in discussion knowest thou not that it is a God whom thou feedest, a God whom thou exercisest, a God whom thou bearest about with thee, O miserable! and thou perceivest it not. Thinkest thou that I speak of a God of silver or gold, that is without thee? Nay, thou bearest Him within thee! all unconscious of polluting Him with thoughts impure and unclean deeds. Were an image of God present, thou wouldest not dare to act as thou dost, yet, when God Himself is present within thee, beholding and hearing all, thou dost not blush to think such thoughts and do such deeds, O thou that art insensible of thine own nature and liest under the wrath of God!

LXI

Why then are we afraid when we send a young man from the Schools into active life, lest he should indulge his appetites intemperately, lest he should debase himself by ragged clothing, or be puffed up by fine raiment? Knows he not the God within him; knows he not with whom he is starting on his way? Have we patience to hear him say to us, Would I had thee with me!—Hast thou not God where thou art, and having Him dost thou still seek for any other! Would He tell thee aught else than these things? Why, wert thou a statue of Phidias, an Athena or a Zeus, thou wouldst bethink thee both of thyself and thine artificer; and hadst thou any sense, thou wouldst strive to do no dishonour to thyself or him that fashioned thee, nor appear to beholders in unbefitting guise. But now, because God is thy Maker, is that why thou carest not of what sort thou shalt show thyself to be? Yet how different the artists and their workmanship! What human artist's work, for example, has in it the faculties that are displayed in fashioning it? Is it aught but marble, bronze, gold, or ivory? Nay, when the Athena of Phidias has put forth her hand and received therein a Victory, in that attitude she stands for evermore. But God's works move and breathe; they use and judge the things of sense. The workmanship of such an Artist, wilt thou dishonor Him? Ay, when he not only fashioned thee, but placed thee, like a ward, in the care and guardianship of thyself alone, wilt thou not only forget this, but also do dishonour to what is committed to thy care! If God had entrusted thee with an orphan, wouldst thou have thus neglected him? He hath delivered thee to thine own care, saying, I had none more faithful than myself: keep this man for me such as Nature hath made him—modest, faithful, high-minded, a stranger to fear, to passion, to perturbation....

Such will I show myself to you all.—"What, exempt from sickness also: from age, from death?"—Nay, but accepting sickness, accepting death as becomes a God!

LXII

No labour, according to Diogenes, is good but that which aims at producing courage and strength of soul rather than of body.

LXIII

A guide, on finding a man who has lost his way, brings him back to the right path—he does not mock and jeer at him and then take himself off. You also must show the unlearned man the truth, and you will see that he will follow. But so long as you do not show it him, you should not mock, but rather feel your own incapacity.

LXIV

It was the first and most striking characteristic of Socrates never to become heated in discourse, never to utter an injurious or insulting word—on the contrary, he persistently bore insult from others and thus put an end to the fray. If you care to know the extent of his power in this direction, read Xenophon's Banquet, and you will see how many quarrels he put an end to. This is why the Poets are right in so highly commending this faculty:—

Quickly and wisely withal even bitter feuds would he settle.

Nevertheless the practice is not very safe at present, especially in Rome. One who adopts it, I need not say, ought not to carry it out in an obscure corner, but boldly accost, if occasion serve, some personage of rank or wealth.

"Can you tell me, sir, to whose care you entrust your horses?"

"I can."

"Is it to the first comer, who knows nothing about them?"

"Certainly not."

"Well, what of the man who takes care of your gold, your silver or your raiment?"

"He must be experienced also."

"And your body—have you ever considered about entrusting it to any one's care?"

"Of course I have."

"And no doubt to a person of experience as a trainer, a physician?"

"Surely."

"And these things the best you possess, or have you anything more precious?"

"What can you mean?"

"I mean that which employs these; which weights all things; which takes counsel and resolve."

"Oh, you mean the soul."

"You take me rightly; I do mean the soul. By Heaven, I hold that far more precious than all else I possess. Can you show me then what care you bestow on a soul? For it can scarcely be thought that a man of your wisdom and consideration in the city would suffer your most precious possession to go to ruin through carelessness and neglect."

"Certainly not."

"Well, do you take care of it yourself? Did any one teach you the right method, or did you discover it yourself?"

Now here comes in the danger: first, that the great man may

answer, "Why, what is that to you, my good fellow? are you my master?" And then, if you persist in troubling him, may raise his hand to strike you. It is a practice of which I was myself a warm admirer until such experiences as these befell me.

LXV

When a youth was giving himself airs in the Theatre and saying, "I am wise, for I have conversed with many wise men," Epictetus replied, "I too have conversed with many rich men, yet I am not rich!"

LXVI

We see that a carpenter becomes a carpenter by learning certain things: that a pilot, by learning certain things, becomes a pilot. Possibly also in the present case the mere desire to be wise and good is not enough. It is necessary to learn certain things. This is then the object of our search. The Philosophers would have us first learn that there is a God, and that His Providence directs the Universe; further, that to hide from Him not only one's acts but even one's thoughts and intentions is impossible; secondly, what the nature of God is. Whatever that nature is discovered to be, the man who would please and obey Him must strive with all his might to be made like unto him. If the Divine is faithful, he also must be faithful; if free, he also must be free; if beneficent, he also must be beneficent; if magnanimous, he also must be magnanimous. Thus as an imitator of God must he follow Him in every deed and word.

LXVII

If I show you, that you lack just what is most important and necessary to happiness, that hitherto your attention has been bestowed on everything rather than that which claims it most; and, to crown all, that you know neither what God nor Man is—neither what Good or Evil is: why, that you are ignorant of everything else, perhaps you may bear to be told; but to hear that you know nothing of yourself, how could you submit to that? How could you stand your ground and suffer that to be proved? Clearly not at all. You instantly turn away in wrath. Yet what harm have I done to you? Unless indeed the mirror harms the ill-favoured man by showing him to himself just as he is; unless the physician can be thought to insult his patient, when he tells him:—"Friend, do you suppose there is nothing wrong with you? why, you have a fever. Eat nothing to-day, and drink only water." Yet no one says, "What an insufferable insult!" Whereas if you say to a man, "Your desires are inflamed, your instincts of rejection are weak and low, your aims are inconsistent, your impulses are not in harmony with Nature, your opinions are rash and false," he forthwith goes away and complains that you have insulted him.

LXVIII

Our way of life resembles a fair. The flocks and herds are passing along to be sold, and the greater part of the crowd to buy and sell. But there are some few who come only to look at the fair, to inquire how and why it is being held, upon what authority and with what object. So too, in this great Fair of life, some, like the cattle, trouble themselves about nothing but the fodder. Know all of you, who are busied about land, slaves and public posts, that these are nothing but fodder! Some few there are attending the Fair, who love to contemplate what the world is, what He that administers it. Can there be no Administrator? is it possible, that while neither city nor household could endure even a moment without one to administer and see to its welfare, this Fabric, so fair, so vast, should be administered in order so harmonious, without a purpose and by blind chance? There is therefore an Administrator. What is His nature and how does He administer? And who are we that are His children and what work were we born to perform? Have we any close connection or relation with Him or not?

Such are the impressions of the few of whom I speak. And further, they apply themselves solely to considering and examining the great assembly before they depart. Well, they are derided by the multitude. So are the lookers-on by the traders: aye, and if the beasts had any sense, they would deride those who thought much of anything but fodder!

LXIX

I think I know now what I never knew before—the meaning of the common saying, A fool you can neither bend nor break. Pray heaven I may never have a wise fool for my friend! There is nothing more intractable.—"My resolve is fixed!"—Why so madman say too; but the more firmly they believe in their delusions, the more they stand in need of treatment.

LXX

—"O! when shall I see Athens and its Acropolis again?"—Miserable man! art thou not contented with the daily sights that meet thine eyes? canst thou behold aught greater or nobler than the Sun, Moon, and Stars; than the outspread Earth and Sea? If indeed thou apprehendest Him who administers the universe, if thou bearest Him about within thee, canst thou still hanker after mere fragments of stone and fine rock? When thou art about to bid farewell to the Sun and Moon itself, wilt thou sit down and cry like a child? Why, what didst thou hear, what didst thou learn? why didst thou write thyself down a philosopher, when thou mightest have written what was the fact, namely, "I have made one or two Compendiums, I have read some works of Chrysippus, and I have not even touched the hem of Philosophy's robe!"

LXXI

Friend, lay hold with a desperate grasp, ere it is too late, on Freedom, on Tranquility, on Greatness of soul! Lift up thy head, as one escaped from slavery; dare to look up to God, and say:—"Deal with me henceforth as Thou wilt; Thou and I are of one mind. I am Thine: I refuse nothing that seeeth good to Thee; lead on whither Thou wilt; clothe me in what garb Thou pleasest; wilt Thou have me a ruler or a subject—at home or in exile—poor or rich? All these things will I justify unto men for Thee. I will show the true nature of each...."

Who would Hercules have been had he loitered at home? no Hercules, but Eurystheus. And in his wanderings through the world how many friends and comrades did he find? but nothing dearer to him than God. Wherefore he was believed to be God's son, as indeed he was. So then in obedience to Him, he went about delivering the earth from injustice and lawlessness.

But thou art not Hercules, thou sayest, and canst not deliver others from their iniquity—not even Theseus, to deliver the soil of Attica from its monsters? Purge away thine own, cast forth thence—from thine own mind, not robbers and monsters, but Fear, Desire, Envy, Malignity, Avarice, Effeminacy, Intemperance. And these may not be cast out, except by looking to God alone, by fixing thy affections on Him only, and by consecrating thyself to His commands. If thou choosest aught else, with sighs and groans thou wilt be forced to follow a Might greater than thine own, ever seeking Tranquillity without, and never able to attain unto her. For thou seekest her where she is not to be found; and where she is, there thou seekest her not!

LXXII

If a man would pursue Philosophy, his first task is to throw away conceit. For it is impossible for a man to begin to learn what he has a conceit that he already knows.

LXXIII

Give me but one young man, that has come to the School with this intention, who stands forth a champion of this cause, and says, "All else I renounce, content if I am but able to pass my life free from hindrance and trouble; to raise my head aloft and face all things as a free man; to look up to heaven as a friend of God, fearing nothing that may come to pass!" Point out such a one to me, that I may say, "Enter, young man, into possession of that which is thine own. For thy lot is to adorn Philosophy. Thine are these possessions; thine these books, these discourses!"

And when our champion has duly exercised himself in this part of the subject, I hope he will come back to me and say:—"What I desire is to be free from passion and from perturbation; as one who grudges no pains in the pursuit of piety and philosophy, what I desire is to know my duty to the Gods, my duty to my parents, to my brothers, to my country, to strangers."

"Enter then on the second part of the subject; it is thine also."

"But I have already mastered the second part; only I wished to stand firm and unshaken—as firm when asleep as when awake, as firm when elated with wine as in despondency and dejection."

"Friend, you are verily a God! you cherish great designs."

LXXIV

"The question at stake," said Epictetus, "is no common one; it is this:—Are we in our senses, or are we not?"

LXXV

If you have given way to anger, be sure that over and above the evil involved therein, you have strengthened the habit, and added fuel to the fire. If overcome by a temptation of the flesh, do not reckon it a single defeat, but that you have also strengthened your dissolute habits. Habits and faculties are necessarily affected by the corresponding acts. Those that were not there before, spring up: the rest gain in strength and extent. This is the account which Philosophers give of the origin of diseases of the mind:—Suppose you have once lusted after money: if reason sufficient to produce a sense of evil be applied, then the lust is checked, and the mind at once regains its original authority; whereas if you have recourse to no remedy, you can no longer look for this return—on the contrary, the next time it is excited by the corresponding object, the flame of desire leaps up more quickly than before. By frequent repetition, the mind in the long run becomes callous; and thus this mental disease produces confirmed Avarice.

One who has had fever, even when it has left him, is not in the same condition of health as before, unless indeed his cure is complete. Something of the same sort is true also of diseases of the mind. Behind, there remains a legacy of traces and blisters: and unless these are effectually erased, subsequent blows on the same spot will produce no longer mere blisters, but sores. If you do not wish to be prone to anger, do not feed the habit; give it nothing which may tend its increase. At first, keep quiet and count the days when you were not angry: "I used to be angry every day, then every other day: next every two, next every three days!" and if you succeed in passing thirty days, sacrifice to the Gods in thanksgiving.

LXXVI

How then may this be attained?—Resolve, now if never before, to approve thyself to thyself; resolve to show thyself fair in God's sight; long to be pure with thine own pure self and God!

LXXVII

That is the true athlete, that trains himself to resist such outward impressions as these.

"Stay, wretched man! suffer not thyself to be carried away!" Great is the combat, divine the task! you are fighting for Kingship, for Liberty, for Happiness, for Tranquillity. Remember God: call upon Him to aid thee, like a comrade that stands beside thee in the fight.

LXXVIII

Who then is a Stoic—in the sense that we call a statue of Phidias which is modelled after that master's art? Show me a man in this sense modelled after the doctrines that are ever upon his lips. Show me a man that is sick—and happy; an exile—and happy; in evil report—and happy! Show me him, I ask again. So help me Heaven, I long to see one Stoic! Nay, if you cannot show me one fully modelled, let me at least see one in whom the process is at work—one whose bent is in that direction. Do me that favour! Grudge it not to an old man, to behold a sight he has never yet beheld. Think you I wish to see the Zeus or Athena of Phidias, bedecked with gold and ivory?—Nay, show me, one of you, a human soul, desiring to be of one mind with God, no more to lay blame on God or man, to suffer nothing to disappoint, nothing to cross him, to yield neither to anger, envy, nor jealousy—in a word, why disguise the matter? one that from a man would fain become a God; one that while still imprisoned in this dead body makes fellowship with God his aim. Show me him!—Ah, you cannot! Then why mock yourselves and delude others? why stalk about tricked out in other men's attire, thieves and robbers that you are of names and things to which you can show no title!

LXXIX

If you have assumed a character beyond your strength, you have both played a poor figure in that, and neglected one that is within your powers.

LXXX

Fellow, you have come to blows at home with a slave: you have turned the household upside down, and thrown the neighbourhood into confusion; and do you come to me then with airs of assumed modesty—do you sit down like a sage and criticise my explanation of the readings, and whatever idle babble you say has come into my head? Have you come full of envy, and dejected because nothing is sent you from home; and while the discussion is going on, do you sit brooding on nothing but how your father or your brother are disposed towards you:—"What are they saying about me there? at this moment they imagine I am making progress and saying, He will return perfectly omniscient! I wish I could become omniscient before I return; but that would be very troublesome. No one sends me anything—the baths at Nicopolis are dirty; things are wretched at home and wretched here." And then they say, "Nobody is any the better for the School."—Who comes to the School with a sincere wish to learn: to submit his principles to correction and himself to treatment? Who, to gain a sense of his wants? Why then be surprised if you carry home from the School exactly what you bring into it?

LXXXI

"Epictetus, I have often come desiring to hear you speak, and you have never given me any answer; now if possible, I entreat you, say something to me."

"Is there, do you think," replied Epictetus, "an art of speaking as of other things, if it is to be done skilfully and with profit to the hearer?"

"Yes."

"And are all profited by what they hear, or only some among them? So that it seems there is an art of hearing as well as of speaking.... To make a statue needs skill: to view a statue aright needs skill also."

"Admitted."

"And I think all will allow that one who proposes to hear philosophers speak needs a considerable training in hearing. Is that not so? The tell me on what subject your are able to hear me."

"Why, on good and evil."

"The good and evil of what? a horse, an ox?"

"No; of a man."

"Do we know then what Man is? what his nature is? what is the idea we have of him? And are our ears practised in any degree on the subject? Nay, do you understand what Nature is? can you follow me in any degree when I say that I shall have to use demonstration? Do you understand what Demonstration is? what True or False is? ... must I drive you to Philosophy? ... Show me what good I am to do by discoursing with you. Rouse my desire to do so. The sight of a pasture it loves stirs in a sheep the desire to feed: show it a stone or a bit of bread and it remains unmoved. Thus we also have certain natural desires, aye, and one that moves us to speak when we find a listener that is worth his salt: one that himself stirs the spirit. But if he sits by like a stone or a tuft of grass, how can he rouse a man's desire?"

"Then you will say nothing to me?"

"I can only tell you this: that one who knows not who he is and to what end he was born; what kind of world this is and with whom he is associated therein; one who cannot distinguish Good and Evil, Beauty and Foulness, ... Truth and Falsehood, will never follow Reason in shaping his desires and impulses and repulsions, nor yet in assent, denial, or suspension of judgement; but will in one word go about deaf and blind, thinking himself to be somewhat, when he is in truth of no account. Is there anything new in all this? Is not this ignorance the cause of all the mistakes and mischances of men since the human race began? . . ."

"This is all I have to say to you, and even this against the grain. Why? Because you have not stirred my spirit. For what can I see in you to stir me, as a spirited horse will stir a judge of horses? Your body? That you maltreat. Your dress? That is luxurious. You behavior, your look?—Nothing whatever. When you want to hear a philosopher, do not say, You say nothing to me'; only show yourself worthy or fit to hear, and then you will see how you will move the speaker."

LXXXII

And now, when you see brothers apparently good friends and living in accord, do not immediately pronounce anything upon their friendship, though they should affirm it with an oath, though they should declare, "For us to live apart in a thing impossible!" For the heart of a bad man is faithless, unprincipled, inconstant: now overpowered by one impression, now by another. Ask not the usual questions, Were they born of the same parents, reared together, and under the same tutor; but ask this only, in what they place their real interest—whether in outward things or in the Will. If in outward things, call them not friends, any more than faithful, constant, brave or free: call them not even human beings, if you have any sense. . . . But should you hear that these men hold the Good to lie only in the Will, only in rightly dealing with the things of sense, take no more trouble to inquire whether they are father and son or brothers, or comrades of long standing; but, sure of this one thing, pronounce as boldly that they are friends as that they are faithful and just: for where else can Friendship be found than where Modesty is, where there is an interchange of things fair and honest, and of such only?

LXXXIII

No man can rob us of our Will—no man can lord it over that!

LXXXIV

When disease and death overtake me, I would fain be found engaged in the task of liberating mine own Will from the assaults of passion, from hindrance, from resentment, from slavery.

Thus would I fain to be found employed, so that I may say to God, "Have I in aught transgressed Thy commands? Have I in aught perverted the faculties, the senses, the natural principles that Thou didst give me? Have I ever blamed Thee or found fault with Thine administration? When it was Thy good pleasure, I fell sick—and so did other men: by my will consented. Because it was Thy pleasure, I became poor: but my heart rejoiced. No power in the State was mine, because Thou wouldst not: such power I never desired! Hast Thou ever seen me of more doleful countenance on that account? Have I not ever drawn nigh unto Thee with cheerful look, waiting upon Thy commands, attentive to Thy signals? Wilt Thou that I now depart from the great Assembly of men? I go: I give Thee all thanks, that Thou hast deemed me worthy to take part with Thee in this Assembly: to behold Thy works, to comprehend this Thine administration."

Such I would were the subject of my thoughts, my pen, my study, when death overtakes me.

LXXXV

Seemeth it nothing to you, never to accuse, never to blame either God or Man? to wear ever the same countenance in going forth as in coming in? This was the secret of Socrates: yet he never said that he knew or taught anything. . . . Who amongst you makes this his aim? Were it indeed so, you would gladly endure sickness, hunger, aye, death itself.

LXXXVI

How are we constituted by Nature? To be free, to be noble, to be modest (for what other living thing is capable of blushing, or of feeling the impression of shame?) and to subordinate pleasure to the ends for which Nature designed us, as a handmaid and a minister, in order to call forth our activity; in order to keep us constant to the path prescribed by Nature.

LXXXVII

The husbandman deals with land; physicians and trainers with the body; the wise man with his own Mind.

LXXXVIII

Which of us does not admire what Lycurgus the Spartan did? A young citizen had put out his eye, and been handed over to him by the people to be punished at his own discretion. Lycurgus abstained from all vengeance, but on the contrary instructed and made a good man of him. Producing him in public in the theatre, he said to the astonished Spartans:—"I received this young man at your hands full of violence and wanton insolence; I restore him to you in his right mind and fit to serve his country."

LXXXIX

A money-changer may not reject Cæsar's coin, nor may the seller of herbs, but must when once the coin is shown, deliver what is sold for it, whether he will or no. So is it also with the Soul. Once the Good appears, it attracts towards itself; evil repels. But a clear and certain impression of the Good the Soul will never reject, any more than men do Cæsar's coin. On this hangs every impulse alike of Man and God.

XC

Asked what Common Sense was, Epictetus replied:—
As that may be called a Common Ear which distinguishes only sounds, while that which distinguishes musical notes is not common but produced by training; so there are certain things which men not entirely perverted see by the natural principles common to all. Such a constitution of the Mind is called Common Sense.

XCI

Canst thou judge men? . . . then make us imitators of thyself, as Socrates did. Do this, do not do that, else will I cast thee into prison; this is not governing men like reasonable creatures. Say rather, As God hath ordained, so do; else thou wilt suffer chastisement and loss. Askest thou what loss? None other than this: To have left undone what thou shouldst have done: to have lost the faithfulness, the reverence, the modesty that is in thee!

Greater loss than this seek not to find!

XCII

"His son is dead."
What has happened?
"His son is dead."
Nothing more?
"Nothing."
"His ship is lost."
"He has been haled to prison."
What has happened?
"He has been haled to prison."

But that any of these things are misfortunes to him, is an addition which every one makes of his own. But (you say) God is unjust is this.—Why? For having given thee endurance and greatness of soul? For having made such things to be no evils? For placing happiness within thy reach, even when enduring them? For open unto thee a door, when things make not for thy good?—Depart, my friend and find fault no more!

XCIII

You are sailing to Rome (you tell me) to obtain the post of Governor of Cnossus. You are not content to stay at home with the honours you had before; you want something on a larger scale, and more conspicuous. But when did you ever undertake a voyage for the purpose of reviewing your own principles and getting rid of any of them that proved unsound? Whom did you ever visit for that object? What time did you ever set yourself for that? What age? Run over the times of your life—by yourself, if you are ashamed before me. Did you examine your principles when a boy? Did you not do everything just as you do now? Or when you were a stripling, attending the school of oratory and practising the art yourself, what did you ever imagine you lacked? And when you were a young man, entered upon public life, and were pleading causes and making a name, who any longer seemed equal to you? And at what moment would you have endured another examining your principles and proving that they were unsound? What then am I to say to you? "Help me in this matter!" you cry. Ah, for that I have no rule! And neither did you, if that was your object, come to me as a philosopher, but as you might have gone to a herb-seller or a cobbler.—"What do philosophers have rules for, then?"—Why, that whatever may betide, our ruling faculty may be as Nature would have it, and so remain. Think you this a small matter? Not so! but the greatest thing there is. Well, does it need but a short time? Can it be grasped by a passer-by?—grasp it, if you can!

Then you will say, "Yes, I met Epictetus!"

Aye, just as you might a statue or a monument. You saw me! and that is all. But a man who meets a man is one who learns the other's mind, and lets him see his in turn. Learn my mind— show me yours; and then go and say that you met me. Let us try each other; if I have any wrong principle, rid me of it; if you have, out with it. That is what meeting a philosopher means. Not so, you think; this is only a flying visit; while we are hiring the ship, we can see Epictetus too! Let us see what he has to say. Then on leaving you cry, "Out on Epictetus for a worthless fellow, provincial and barbarous of speech!" What else indeed did you come to judge of?

XCIV

Whether you will or no, you are poorer than I!

"What then do I lack?"

What you have not: Constancy of mind, such as Nature would have it be: Tranquillity. Patron or no patron, what care I? but you do care. I am richer than you: I am not racked with anxiety as to what Cæsar may think of me; I flatter none on that account. This is what I have, instead of vessels of gold and silver! your vessels may be of gold, but your reason, your principles, your accepted views, your inclinations, your desires are of earthenware.

XCV

To you, all you have seems small: to me, all I have seems great. Your desire is insatiable, mine is satisfied. See children thrusting their hands into a narrow-necked jar, and striving to pull out the nuts and figs it contains: if they fill the hand, they cannot pull it out again, and then they fall to tears.—"Let go a few of them, and then you can draw out the rest!"—You, too, let your desire go! covet not many things, and you will obtain.

XCVI

Pittacus wronged by one whom he had it in his power to punish, let him go free, saying, Forgiveness is better than revenge. The one shows native gentleness, the other savagery.

XCVII

"My brother ought not to have treated me thus."
True: but he must see to that. However he may treat me, I must deal rightly by him. This is what lies with me, what none can hinder.

XCVIII

Nevertheless a man should also be prepared to be sufficient

unto himself—to dwell with himself alone, even as God dwells with Himself alone, shares His repose with none, and considers the nature of His own administration, intent upon such thoughts as are meet unto Himself. So should we also be able to converse with ourselves, to need none else beside, to sigh for no distraction, to bend our thoughts upon the Divine Administration, and how we stand related to all else; to observe how human accidents touched us of old, and how they touch us now; what things they are that still have power to hurt us, and how they may be cured or removed; to perfect what needs perfecting as Reason would direct.

XCIX

If a man has frequent intercourse with others, either in the way of conversation, entertainment, or simple familiarity, he must either become like them, or change them to his own fashion. A live coal placed next a dead one will either kindle that or be quenched by it. Such being the risk, it is well to be cautious in admitting intimacies of this sort, remembering that one cannot rub shoulders with a soot-stained man without sharing the soot oneself. What will you do, supposing the talk turns on gladiators, or horses, or prize-fighters, or (what is worse) on persons, condemning this and that, approving the other? Or suppose a man sneers and jeers or shows a malignant temper? Has any among us the skill of the lute-player, who knows at the first touch which strings are out of tune and sets the instrument right: has any of you such power as Socrates had, in all his intercourse with men, of winning them over to his own convictions? Nay, but you must needs be swayed hither and thither by the uninstructed. How comes it then that they prove so much stronger than you? Because they speak from the fulness of the heart—their low, corrupt views are their real convictions: whereas your fine sentiments are but from the lips, outwards; that is why they are so nerveless and dead. It turns one's stomach to listen to your exhortations, and hear of your miserable Virtue, that you prate of up and down. Thus it is that the Vulgar prove too strong for you.

Everywhere strength, everywhere victory waits your conviction!

C

In general, any methods of discipline applied to the body which tend to modify its desires or repulsions, are good—for ascetic ends. But if done for display, they betray at once a man who keeps an eye on outward show; who has an ulterior purpose, and is looking for spectators to shout, "Oh what a great man!" This is why Apollonius so well said: "If you are bent upon a little private discipline, wait till you are choking with heat some day—then take a mouthful of cold water, and spit it out again, and tell no man!"

CI

Study how to give as one that is sick: that thou mayest hereafter give as one that is whole. Fast; drink water only; abstain altogether from desire, that thou mayest hereafter conform thy desire to Reason.

CII

Thou wouldst do good unto men? then show them by thine own example what kind of men philosophy can make, and cease from foolish trifling. Eating, do good to them that eat with thee; drinking, to them that drink with thee; yield unto all, give way, and bear with them. Thus shalt thou do them good: but vent not upon them thine own evil humour!

CIII

Even as bad actors cannot sing alone, but only in chorus: so some cannot walk alone.

Man, if thou art aught, strive to walk alone and hold converse with thyself, instead of skulking in the chorus! at length think; look around thee; bestir thyself, that thou mayest know who thou art!

CIV

You would fain be victor at the Olympic games, you say. Yes, but weigh the conditions, weigh the consequences; then and then only, lay to your hand—if it be for your profit. You must live by rule, submit to diet, abstain from dainty meats, exercise your body perforce at stated hours, in heat or in cold; drink no cold water, nor, it may be, wine. In a word, you must surrender yourself wholly to your trainer, as though to a physician.

Then in the hour of contest, you will have to delve the ground, it may chance dislocate an arm, sprain an ankle, gulp down abundance of yellow sand, be scourge with the whip—and with all this sometimes lose the victory. Count the cost—and then, if your desire still holds, try the wrestler's life. Else let me tell you that you will be behaving like a pack of children playing now at wrestlers, now at gladiators; presently falling to trumpeting and anon to stage-playing, when the fancy takes them for what they have seen. And you are even the same: wrestler, gladiator, philosopher, orator all by turns and none of them with your whole soul. Like an ape, you mimic what you see, to one thing constant never; the thing that is familiar charms no more. This is because you never undertook aught with due consideration, nor after strictly testing and viewing it from every side; no, your choice was thoughtless; the glow of your desire had waxed cold....

Friend, bethink you first what it is you would do, and then what your own nature is able to bear. Would you be a wrestler, consider your shoulders, your thighs, your loins—not all men are formed to the same end. Think you to be a philosopher while acting as you do? think you go on thus eating, thus drinking, giving way in like manner to wrath and to displeasure? Nay, you must watch, you must labour; overcome certain desires; quit your familiar friends, submit to be despised by your slave, to be held in derision by them that meet you, to take the lower place in all things, in office, in positions of authority, in courts of law.

Weigh these things fully, and then, if you will, lay to your hand; if as the price of these things you would gain Freedom, Tranquillity, and passionless Serenity.

CV

He that hath no musical instruction is a child in Music; he that hath no letters is a child in Learning; he that is untaught is a child in Life.

CVI

Can any profit be derived from these men? Aye, from all.
"What, even from a reviler?"
Why, tell me what profit a wrestler gains from him who exercises him beforehand? The very greatest: he trains me in the practice of endurance, of controlling my temper, of gentle ways. You deny it. What, the man who lays hold of my neck, and disciplines loins and shoulders, does me good, ... while he that trains me to keep my temper does me none? This is what it means, not knowing how to gain advantage from men! Is my neighbour bad? Bad to himself, but good to me: he brings my good temper, my gentleness into play. Is my father bad? Bad to himself, but good to me. This is the rod of Hermes; touch what you will with it, they say, and it becomes gold. Nay, but bring what you will and I will transmute it into Good. Bring sickness, bring death,

bring poverty and reproach, bring trial for life—all these things through the rod of Hermes shall be turned to profit.

CVII

Till then these sound opinions have taken firm root in you, and you have gained a measure of strength for your security, I counsel you to be cautious in associating with the uninstructed. Else whatever impressions you receive upon the tablets of your mind in the School will day by day melt and disappear, like wax in the sun. Withdraw then somewhere far from the sun, while you have these waxen sentiments.

CVIII

We must approach this matter in a different way; it is great and mystical: it is no common thing; nor given to every man. Wisdom alone, it may be, will not suffice for the care of youth: a man needs also a certain measure of readiness—an aptitude for the office; aye, and certain bodily qualities; and above all, to be counselled of God Himself to undertake this post; even as He counselled Socrates to fill the post of one who confutes error, assigning to Diogenes the royal office of high reproof, and to Zeno that of positive instruction. Whereas you would fain set up for a physician provided with nothing but drugs! Where and how they should be applied you neither know nor care.

CIX

If what charms you is nothing but abstract principles, sit down and turn them over quietly in your mind: but never dub yourself a Philosopher, nor suffer others to call you so. Say rather: He is in error; for my desires, my impulses are unaltered. I give in my adhesion to what I did before; nor has my mode of dealing with the things of sense undergone any change.

CX

When a friend inclined to Cynic views asked Epictetus, what sort of person a true Cynic should be, requesting a general sketch of the system, he answered:—"We will consider that at leisure. At present I content myself with saying this much: If a man put his hand to so weighty a matter without God, the wrath of God abides upon him. That which he covets will but bring upon him public shame. Not even on finding himself in a well-ordered house does a man step forward and say to himself, I must be master here! Else the lord of that house takes notice of it, and, seeing him insolently giving orders, drags him forth and chastises him. So it is also in this great City, the World. Here also is there a Lord of the House, who orders all thing:—

"Thou are the Sun! in thine orbit thou hast
power to make the year and the seasons;
to bid the fruits of the earth to grow
and increase, the winds arise and fall;
thou canst in due measure cherish with
thy warmth the frames of men; go make
thy circuit, and thus minister unto all
from the greatest to the least! . . ."

"Thou canst lead a host against Troy; be Agamemnon!"

"Thou canst meet Hector in single combat; be Achilles!"

"But had Thersites stepped forward and claimed the chief command, he had been met with a refusal, or obtained it only to his own shame and confusion of face, before a cloud of witnesses."

CXI

Others may fence themselves with walls and houses, when they do such deeds as these, and wrap themselves in darkness—aye, they have many a device to hide themselves. Another may shut his door and station one before his chamber to say, if any comes, He has gone forth! he is not at leisure! But the true Cynic will have none of these things; instead of them, he must wrap himself in Modesty: else he will but bring himself to shame, naked and under the open sky. That is his house; that is his door; that is the slave that guards his chamber; that is his darkness!

CXII

Death? let it come when it will, whether it smite but a part of the whole: Fly, you tell me—fly! But whither shall I fly? Can any man cast me beyond the limits of the World? It may not be! And whithersoever I go, there shall I still find Sun, Moon, and Stars; there I shall find dreams, and omens, and converse with the Gods!

CXIII

Furthermore the true Cynic must know that he is sent as a Messenger from God to men, to show unto them that as touching good and evil they are in error; looking for these where they are not to be found, nor ever bethinking themselves where they are. And like Diogenes when brought before Philip after the battle of Chaeronea, the Cynic must remember that he is a Spy. For a Spy he really is—to bring back word what things are on Man's side, and what against him. And when he had diligently observed all, he must come back with a true report, not terrified into announcing them to be foes that are no foes, nor otherwise perturbed or confounded by the things of sense.

CXIV

How can it be that one who hath nothing, neither raiment, nor house, nor home, nor bodily tendance, nor servant, nor city, should yet live tranquil and contented? Behold God hath sent you a man to show you in act and deed that it may be so. Behold me! I have neither house nor possessions nor servants: the ground is my couch; I have no wife, no children, no shelter—nothing but earth and sky, and one poor cloak. And what lack I yet? am I not untouched by sorrow, by fear? am I not free? . . . when have I laid anything to the charge of God or Man? when have I accused any? hath any of you seen me with a sorrowful countenance? And in what wise treat I those of whom you stand in fear and awe? Is it not as slaves? Who when he seeth me doth not think that he beholdeth his Master and his King?

CXV

Give thyself more diligently to reflection: know thyself: take counsel with the Godhead: without God put thine hand unto nothing!

CXVI

"But to marry and to rear offspring," said the young man, "will the Cynic hold himself bound to undertake this as a chief duty?"

Grant me a republic of wise men, answered Epictetus, and

perhaps none will lightly take the Cynic life upon him. For on whose account should he embrace that method of life? Suppose however that he does, there will then be nothing to hinder his marrying and rearing offspring. For his wife will be even such another as himself, and likewise her father; and in like manner will his children be brought up.

But in the present condition of things, which resembles an Army in battle array, ought not the Cynic to be free from all distraction and given wholly to the service of God, so that he can go in and out among men, neither fettered by the duties nor entangled by the relations of common life? For if he transgress them, he will forfeit the character of a good man and true; whereas if he observe them, there is an end to him as the Messenger, the Spy, the Herald of the Gods!

CXVII

Ask me if you choose if a Cynic shall engage in the administration of the State. O fool, seek you a nobler administration that that in which he is engaged? Ask you if a man shall come forward in the Athenian assembly and talk about revenue and supplies, when his business is to converse with all men, Athenians, Corinthians, and Romans alike, not about supplies, not about revenue, nor yet peace and war, but about Happiness and Misery, Prosperity and Adversity, Slavery and Freedom?

Ask you whether a man shall engage in the administration of the State who has engaged in such an Administration as this? Ask me too if he shall govern; and again I will answer, Fool, what greater government shall he hold than he holds already?

CXVIII

Such a man needs also to have a certain habit of body. If he appears consumptive, thin and pale, his testimony has no longer the same authority. He must not only prove to the unlearned by showing them what his Soul is that it is possible to be a good man apart from all that they admire; but he must also show them, by his body, that a plain and simple manner of life under the open sky does no harm to the body either. "See, I am proof of this! and my body also." As Diogenes used to do, who went about fresh of look and by the very appearance of his body drew men's eyes. But if a Cynic is an object of pity, he seems a mere beggar; all turn away, all are offended at him. Nor should he be slovenly of look, so as not to scare men from him in this way either; on the contrary, his very roughness should be clean and attractive.

CXIX

Kings and tyrants have armed guards wherewith to chastise certain persons, though they themselves be evil. But to the Cynic conscience gives this power—not arms and guards. When he knows that he has watched and laboured on behalf of mankind: that sleep hath found him pure, and left him purer still: that his thoughts have been the thought of a Friend of the Gods—of a servant, yet one that hath a part in the government of the Supreme God: that the words are ever on his lips:—
Lead me, O God, and thou, O Destiny!
as well as these:—
If this be God's will, so let it be!
Why should he not speak boldly unto his own brethren, unto his children—in a word, unto all that are akin to him!

CXX

Does a Philosopher apply to people to come and hear him? does he not rather, of his own nature, attract those that will be benefited by him—like the sun that warms, the food that sustains them? What Physician applies to men to come and be healed? (Though indeed I hear that the Physicians at Rome do nowadays apply for patients—in my time they were applied to.) I apply to you to come and hear that you are in evil case; that what deserves your attention most is the last thing to gain it; that you know not good from evil, and are in short a hapless wretch; a fine way to apply! though unless the words of the Philosopher affect you thus, speaker and speech are alike dead.

CXXI

A Philosopher's school is a Surgery: pain, not pleasure, you should have felt therein. For on entering none of you is whole. One has a shoulder out of joint, another an abscess: a third suffers from an issue, a fourth from pains in the head. And am I then to sit down and treat you to pretty sentiments and empty flourishes, so that you may applaud me and depart, with neither shoulder, nor head, nor issue, nor abscess a whit the better for your visit? Is it then for this that young men are to quit their homes, and leave parents, friends, kinsmen and substance to mouth out Bravo to your empty phrases!

CXXII

If any be unhappy, let him remember that he is unhappy by reason of himself alone. For God hath made all men to enjoy felicity and constancy of good.

CXXIII

Shall we never wean ourselves—shall we never heed the teachings of Philosophy (unless perchance they have been sounding in our ears like an enchanter's drone):—

This World is one great City, and one is the substance whereof it is fashioned: a certain period indeed there needs must be, while these give place to those; some must perish for others to succeed; some move and some abide: yet all is full of friends—first God, then Men, whom Nature hath bound by ties of kindred each to each.

CXXIV

Nor did the hero weep and lament at leaving his children orphans. For he knew that no man is an orphan, but it is the Father that careth for all continually and for evermore. Not by mere report had he heard that the Supreme God is the Father of men: seeing that he called Him Father believing Him so to be, and in all that he did had ever his eyes fixed upon Him. Wherefore in whatsoever place he was, there is was given him to live happily.

CXXV

Know you not that the thing is a warfare? one man's duty is to mount guard, another must go out to reconnoitre, a third to battle; all cannot be in one place, nor would it even be expedient. But you, instead of executing you Commander's orders, complain if aught harsher than usual is enjoined; not understanding to what condition you are bringing the army, so far as in you lies. If all were to follow your example, none would dig a trench, none would cast a rampart around the camp, none would keep watch, or expose himself to danger; but all turn out useless for the service of war. . . . Thus it is here also. Every life is a warfare, and that long and various. You must fulfil a soldier's duty, and obey each order at your commander's nod: aye, if it be possible, divine what he would have done; for between that Command and this, there is no comparison, either in might or in excellence.

CXXVI

Have you again forgotten? Know you not that a good man does nothing for appearance' sake, but for the sake of having done right? . . .
"Is there no reward then?"
Reward! do you seek any greater reward for a good man than doing what is right and just? Yet at the Great Games you look for nothing else; there the victor's crown you deem enough. Seems it to you so small a thing and worthless, to be a good man, and happy therein?

CXXVII

It befits thee not to be unhappy by reason of any, but rather to be happy by reason of all men, and especially by reason of God, who formed us to this end.

CXXVIII

What, did Diogenes love no man, he that was so gentle, so true a friend to men as cheerfully to endure such bodily hardships for the common weal of all mankind? But how loved he them? As behoved a minister of the Supreme God, alike caring for men and subject unto God.

CXXIX

I am by Nature made for my own good; not for my own evil.

CXXX

Remind thyself that he whom thou lovest is mortal—that what thou lovest is not thine own; it is given thee for the present, not irrevocably nor for ever, but even as a fig or a bunch of grapes at the appointed season of the year. . . .

"But these are words of evil omen.". . .

What, callest thou aught of evil omen save that which signifies some evil thing? Cowardice is a word of evil omen, if thou wilt, and meanness of spirit, and lamentation and mourning, and shamelessness. . . .

But do not, I pray thee, call of evil omen a word that is significant of any natural thing:—as well call of evil omen the reaping of the corn; for that means the destruction of the ears, though not of the World!—as well say that the fall of the leaf is of evil omen; that the dried fig should take the place of the green; that raisins should be made from grapes. All these are changes from a former state into another; not destruction, but an ordered economy, a fixed administration. Such is leaving home, a change of small account; such is Death, a greater change, from what now is, not to what is not, but to what is not now.

"Shall I then no longer be?"

Not so; thou wilt be; but something different, of which the World now hath need. For thou too wert born not when thou chosest, but when the World had need of thee.

CXXXI

Wherefore a good man and true, bearing in mind who he is and whence he came and from whom he sprang, cares only how he may fill his post with due discipline and obedience to God.

Wilt thou that I continue to live? Then will I live, as one that is free and noble, as Thou wouldst have me. For Thou hast made me free from hindrance in what appertaineth unto me. But hast Thou no further need of me? I thank Thee! Up to this hour have I stayed for Thy sake and none other's: and now in obedience to Thee I depart.

"How dost thou depart?"

Again I say, as Thou wouldst have me; as one that is free, as Thy servant, as one whose ear is open unto what Thou dost enjoin, what Thou dost forbid.

CXXXII

Whatsoever place or post Thou assignest me, sooner will I die a thousand deaths, as Socrates said, than desert it. And where wilt Thou have me to be? At Rome or Athens? At Thebes or on a desert island? Only remember me there! Shouldst Thou send me where man cannot live as Nature would have him, I will depart, not in disobedience to Thee, but as though Thou wert sounding the signal for my retreat: I am not deserting Thee—far be that from me! I only perceive that thou needest me no longer.

CXXXIII

If you are in Gyaros, do not let your mind dwell upon life at Rome, and all the pleasures it offered to you when living there, and all that would attend your return. Rather be intent on this—how he that lives in Gyaros may live in Gyaros like a man of spirit. And if you are at Rome, do not let your mind dwell upon the life at Athens, but study only how to live at Rome.

Finally, in the room of all other pleasures put this—the pleasure which springs from conscious obedience to God.

CXXXIV

To a good man there is no evil, either in life or death. And if God supply not food, has He not, as a wise Commander, sounded the signal for retreat and nothing more? I obey, I follow—speaking good of my Commander, and praising His acts. For at His good pleasure I came; and I depart when it pleases Him; and while I was yet alive that was my work, to sing praises unto God!

CXXXV

Reflect that the chief source of all evils to Man, and of baseness and cowardice, is not death, but the fear of death.

Against this fear then, I pray you, harden yourself; to this let all your reasonings, your exercises, your reading tend. Then shall you know that thus alone are men set free.

CXXXVI

He is free who lives as he wishes to live; to whom none can do violence, none hinder or compel; whose impulses are unimpeded, whose desires are attain their purpose, who falls not into what he would avoid. Who then would live in error?—None. Who would live deceived and prone to fall, unjust, intemperate, in abject whining at his lot?—None. Then doth no wicked man live as he would, and therefore neither is he free.

CXXXVII

Thus do the more cautious of travellers act. The road is said to be beset by robbers. The traveller will not venture alone, but awaits the companionship on the road of an ambassador, a quaestor or a proconsul. To him he attaches himself and thus passes by in safety. So doth the wise man in the world. Many are the companies of robbers and tyrants, many the storms, the straits, the losses of all a man holds dearest. Whither shall he fall for refuge—how shall he pass by unassailed? What companion on the road shall he await for protection? Such and such a wealthy man, of consular rank? And how shall I be profited, if he is stripped and falls to lamentation and weeping? And how if my fellow-traveller himself turns upon me and robs me? What am I to do? I will become a friend of Cæsar's! in his train none will do me wrong! In the first place—O the indignities I must endure to win distinction! O the multitude of hands there will be to rob me! And if I succeed, Cæsar too is but a mortal. While should it come to pass that I offend him, whither shall I flee from his presence? To the wilderness? And may not fever await me there? What then is to be done? Cannot a fellow-traveller be found that is honest and loyal, strong and secure against surprise? Thus doth the wise man reason, considering that if he would pass through in safety, he must attach himself unto God.

CXXXVIII

"How understandest thou attach himself to God?"
That what God wills, he should will also; that what God wills not, neither should he will.
"How then may this come to pass?"
By considering the movements of God, and His administration.

CXXXIX

And dost thou that hast received all from another's hands, repine and blame the Giver, if He takes anything from thee? Why, who art thou, and to what end comest thou here? was it not He that made the Light manifest unto thee, that gave thee fellow-workers, and senses, and the power to reason? And how brought He thee into the world? Was it not as one born to die; as one bound to live out his earthly life in some small tabernacle of flesh; to behold His administration, and for a little while share with Him in the mighty march of this great Festival Procession? Now therefore that thou hast beheld, while it was permitted thee, the Solemn Feast and Assembly, wilt thou not cheerfully depart, when He summons thee forth, with adoration and thanksgiving for what thou hast seen and heard?—"Nay, but I would fain have stayed longer at the Festival."—Ah, so would the mystics fain have the rites prolonged; so perchance would the crowd at the Great Games fain behold more wrestlers still. But the Solemn Assembly is over! Come forth, depart with thanksgiving and modesty—give place to others that must come into being even as thyself.

CXL

Why art thou thus insatiable? why thus unreasonable? why encumber the world?—"Aye, but I fain would have my wife and children with me too."—What, are they then thine, and not His that gave them—His that made thee? Give up then that which is not thine own: yield it to One who is better than thou. "Nay, but why did He bring one into the world on these conditions?"—If it suits thee not, depart! He hath no need of a spectator who finds fault with his lot! Them that will take part in the Feast he needeth—that will lift their voices with the rest that men may applaud the more, and exalt the Great Assembly in hymns and songs of praise. But the wretched and the fearful He will not be displeased to see absent from it: for when they were present, they did not behave as at a Feast, nor fulfil their proper office; but moaned as though in pain, and found fault with their fate, their fortune and their companions; insensible to what had fallen to their lot, insensible to the powers they had received for a very different purpose—the powers of Magnanimity, Nobility of Heart, of Fortitude, or Freedom!

CXLI

Art thou then free? a man may say. So help me heaven, I long and pray for freedom! But I cannot look my masters boldly in the face; I still value the poor body; I still set much store on its preservation whole and sound.

But I can point thee out a free man, that thou mayest be no more in search of an example. Diogenes was free. How so? Not because he was of free parentage (for that, indeed, was not the case), but because he was himself free. He had cast away every handle whereby slavery might lay hold of him to enslave him, nor was it possible for any to approach and take hold of him to enslave him. All things sat loose upon him—all things were to him attached by but slender ties. Hadst thou seized upon his possessions, he would rather have let them go than have followed thee for them—aye, had it been even a limb, or mayhap his whole body; and in like manner, relatives, friends, and country. For he knew whence they came—from whose hands and on what terms he had received them. His true forefathers, the Gods, his true Country, he never would have abandoned; nor would he have yielded to any man in obedience and submission to the one nor in cheerfully dying for the other. For he was ever mindful that everything that comes to pass has its source and origin there; being indeed brought about for the weal of that his true Country, and directed by Him in whose governance it is.

CXLII

Ponder on this—on these convictions, on these words: fix

thine eyes on these examples, if thou wouldst be free, if thou hast thine heart set upon the matter according to its worth. And what marvel if thou purchase so great a thing at so great and high a price? For the sake of this that men deem liberty, some hang themselves, others cast themselves down from the rock; aye, time has been when whole cities came utterly to an end: while for the sake of Freedom that is true, and sure, and unassailable, dost thou grudge to God what He gave, when He claims it? Wilt thou not study, as Plato saith, to endure, not death alone, but torture, exile, stripes—in a word, to render up all that is not thine own? Else thou wilt be a slave amid slaves, wert thou ten thousand times a consul; aye, not a whit the less, though thou climb the Palace steps. And thou shalt know how true the saying of Cleanthes, that though the words of philosophers may run counter to the opinions of the world, yet have they reason on their side.

CXLIII

Asked how a man should best grieve his enemy, Epictetus replied, "By setting himself to live the noblest life himself."

CXLIV

I am free, I am a friend of God, ready to render Him willing obedience. Of all else I may set store by nothing—neither by mine own body, nor possessions, nor office, nor good report, nor, in a word, aught else beside. For it is not His Will, that I should so set store by these things. Had it been His pleasure, He would have placed my Good therein. But now He hath not done so: therefore I cannot transgress one jot of His commands. In everything hold fast to that which is thy Good—but to all else (as far as is given thee) within the measure of Reason only, contented with this alone. Else thou wilt meet with failure, ill success, let and hindrance. These are the Laws ordained of God—these are His Edicts; these a man should expound and interpret; to these submit himself, not to the laws of Masurius and Cassius.

CXLV

Remember that not the love of power and wealth sets us under the heel of others, but even the love of tranquillity, of leisure, of change of scene—of learning in general, it matters not what the outward thing may be—to set store by it is to place thyself in subjection to another. Where is the difference then between desiring to be a Senator, and desiring not to be one: between thirsting for office and thirsting to be quit of it? Where is the difference between crying, Woe is me, I know not what to do, bound hand and foot as I am to my books so that I cannot stir! and crying, Woe is me, I have not time to read! As though a book were not as much an outward thing and independent of the will, as office and power and the receptions of the great.

Or what reason hast thou (tell me) for desiring to read? For if thou aim at nothing beyond the mere delight of it, or gaining some scrap of knowledge, thou art but a poor, spiritless knave. But if thou desirest to study to its proper end, what else is this than a life that flows on tranquil and serene? And if thy reading secures thee not serenity, what profits it?—"Nay, but it doth secure it," quoth he, "and that is why I repine at being deprived of it."—And what serenity is this that lies at the mercy of every passer-by? I say not at the mercy of the Emperor or Emperor's favorite, but such as trembles at a raven's croak and piper's din, a fever's touch or a thousand things of like sort! Whereas the life serene has no more certain mark than this, that it ever moves with constant unimpeded flow.

CXLVI

If thou hast put malice and evil speaking from thee, altogether, or in some degree: if thou hast put away from thee rashness, foulness of tongue, intemperance, sluggishness: if thou art not moved by what once moved thee, or in like manner as thou once wert moved—then thou mayest celebrate a daily festival, to-day because thou hast done well in this manner, to-morrow in that. How much greater cause is here for offering sacrifice, than if a man should become Consul or Prefect?

CXLVII

These things hast thou from thyself and from the Gods: only remember who it is that giveth them—to whom and for what purpose they were given. Feeding thy soul on thoughts like these, dost thou debate in what place happiness awaits thee? in what place thou shalt do God's pleasure? Are not the Gods nigh unto all places alike; see they not alike what everywhere comes to pass?

CXLVIII

To each man God hath granted this inward freedom. These are the principles that in a house create love, in a city concord, among nations peace, teaching a man gratitude towards God and cheerful confidence, wherever he may be, in dealing with outward things that he knows are neither his nor worth striving after.

CXLIX

If you seek Truth, you will not seek to gain a victory by every possible means; and when you have found Truth, you need not fear being defeated.

CL.

What foolish talk is this? how can I any longer lay claim to right principles, if I am not content with being what I am, but am all aflutter about what I am supposed to be?

CLI

God hath made all things in the world, nay, the world itself, free from hindrance and perfect, and its parts for the use of the whole. No other creature is capable of comprehending His administration thereof; but the reasonable being Man possesses faculties for the consideration of all these things—not only that he is himself a part, but what part he is, and how it is meet that the parts should give place to the whole. Nor is this all. Being naturally constituted noble, magnanimous, and free, he sees that the things which surround him are of two kinds. Some are free from hindrance and in the power of the will. Other are subject to hindrance, and depend on the will of other men. If then he place his own good, his own best interest, only in that which is free from hindrance and in his power, he will be free, tranquil, happy, unharmed, noble-hearted, and pious; giving thanks to all things unto God, finding fault with nothing that comes to pass, laying no charge against anything. Whereas if he place his good in outward things, depending not on the will, he must perforce be subject to hindrance and restraint, the slave of those that have power over the things he desires and fears; he must perforce be impious, as deeming himself injured at the hands of God; he must be unjust, as ever prone to claim more than his due; he must perforce be of a mean and abject spirit.

CLII

Whom then shall I fear? the lords of the Bedchamber, lest they should shut me out? If they find me desirous of entering in, let them shut me out, if they will.

"Then why comest thou to the door?"

Because I think it meet and right, so long as the Play lasts, to take part therein.

"In what sense art thou then shut out?"

Because, unless I am admitted, it is not my will to enter: on the contrary, my will is simply that which comes to pass. For I esteem what God wills better than what I will. To Him will I cleave as His minister and attendant; having the same movements, the same desires, in a word the same Will as He. There is no such thing as being shut out for me, but only for them that would force their way in.

CLIII

But what says Socrates?—"One man finds pleasure in improving his land, another his horses. My pleasure lies in seeing that I myself grow better day by day."

CLIV

The dress is suited to the craft; the craftsman takes his name from the craft, not from the dress. For this reason Euphrates was right in saying, "I long endeavoured to conceal my following the philosophic life; and this profited me much. In the first place, I knew that what I did aright, I did not for the sake of lookers-on, but for my own. I ate aright—unto myself; I kept the even tenor of my walk, my glance composed and serene—all unto myself and unto God. Then as I fought alone, I was alone in peril. If I did anything amiss or shameful, the cause of Philosophy was not in me endangered; nor did I wrong the multitude by transgressing as a professed philosopher. Wherefore those that knew not my purpose marvelled how it came about, that whilst all my life and conversation was passed with philosophers without exception, I was yet none myself. And what harm that the philosopher should be known by his acts, instead of mere outward signs and symbols?"

CLV

First study to conceal what thou art; seek wisdom a little while unto thyself. Thus grows the fruit; first, the seed must be buried in the earth for a little space; there it must be hid and slowly grow, that it may reach maturity. But if it produce the ear before the jointed stalk, it is imperfect—a thing from the garden of Adonis. Such a sorry growth art thou; thou hast blossomed too soon: the winter cold will wither thee away!

CLVI

First of all, condemn the life thou art now leading: but when thou hast condemned it, do not despair of thyself—be not like them of mean spirit, who once they have yielded, abandon themselves entirely and as it were allow the torrent to sweep them away. No; learn what the wrestling masters do. Has the boy fallen? "Rise," they say, "wrestle again, till thy strength come to thee." Even thus should it be with thee. For know that there is nothing more tractable than the human soul. It needs but to will, and the thing is done; the soul is set upon the right path: as on the contrary it needs but to nod over the task, and all is lost. For ruin and recovery alike are from within.

CLVII

It is the critical moment that shows the man. So when the crisis is upon you, remember that God, like a trainer of wrestlers, has matched you with a rough and stalwart antagonist.—"To what end?" you ask. That you may prove the victor at the Great Games. Yet without toil and sweat this may not be!

CLVIII

If thou wouldst make progress, be content to seem foolish and void of understanding with respect to outward things. Care not to be thought to know anything. If any should make account of thee, distrust thyself.

CLIX

Remember that in life thou shouldst order thy conduct as at a banquet. Has any dish that is being served reached thee? Stretch forth thy hand and help thyself modestly. Doth it pass thee by? Seek not to detain it. Has it not yet come? Send not forth thy desire to meet it, but wait until it reaches thee. Deal thus with children, thus with wife; thus with office, thus with wealth—and one day thou wilt be meet to share the Banquets of the Gods. But if thou dost not so much as touch that which is placed before thee, but despisest it, then shalt thou not only share the Banquets of the Gods, but their Empire also.

CLX

Remember that thou art an actor in a play, and of such sort as the Author chooses, whether long or short. If it be his good pleasure to assign thee the part of a beggar, a ruler, or a simple citizen, thine it is to play it fitly. For thy business is to act the part assigned thee, well: to choose it, is another's.

CLXI

Keep death and exile daily before thine eyes, with all else that men deem terrible, but more especially Death. Then wilt thou never think a mean though, nor covet anything beyond measure.

CLXII

As a mark is not set up in order to be missed, so neither is such a thing as natural evil produced in the World.

CLXIII

Piety toward the Gods, to be sure, consists chiefly in thinking rightly concerning them—that they are, and that they govern the Universe with goodness and justice; and that thou thyself art appointed to obey them, and to submit under all circumstances that arise; acquiescing cheerfully in whatever may happen, sure it is brought to pass and accomplished by the most Perfect Understanding. Thus thou wilt never find fault with the Gods, nor charge them with neglecting thee.

CLXIV

Lose no time in setting before you a certain stamp of character and behaviour both when by yourself and in company with others. Let silence be your general rule; or say only what is necessary and in few words. We shall, however, when occasion demands, enter into discourse sparingly. avoiding common topics as gladiators, horse-races, athletes; and the perpetual talk about food and drink. Above all avoid speaking of persons, either in way of praise or blame, or comparison.

If you can, win over the conversation of your company to what it should be by your own. But if you find yourself cut off without escape among strangers and aliens, be silent.

CLXV

Laughter should not be much, nor frequent, nor unrestrained.

CLXVI

Refuse altogether to take an oath if you can, if not, as far as may be.

CLXVII

Banquets of the unlearned and of them that are without, avoid. But if you have occasion to take part in them, let not your attention be relaxed for a moment, lest you slip after all into evil ways. For you may rest assured that be a man ever so pure himself, he cannot escape defilement if his associates are impure.

CLXVIII

Take what relates to the body as far as the bare use warrants—as meat, drink, raiment, house and servants. But all that makes for show and luxury reject.

CLXIX

If you are told that such an one speaks ill of you, make no defence against what was said, but answer, He surely knew not my other faults, else he would not have mentioned these only!

CLXX

When you visit any of those in power, bethink yourself that you will not find him in: that you may not be admitted: that the door may be shut in your face: that he may not concern himself about you. If with all this, it is your duty to go, bear what happens, and never say to yourself, It was not worth the trouble! For that would smack of the foolish and unlearned who suffer outward things to touch them.

CLXXI

In company avoid frequent and undue talk about your own actions and dangers. However pleasant it may be to you to enlarge upon the risks you have run, others may not find such pleasure in listening to your adventures. Avoid provoking laughter also: it is a habit from which one easily slides into the ways of the foolish, and apt to diminish the respect which your neighbors feel for you. To border on coarse talk is also dangerous. On such occasions, if a convenient opportunity offer, rebuke the speaker. If not, at least by relapsing into silence, colouring, and looking annoyed, show that you are displeased with the subject.

CLXXII

When you have decided that a thing ought to be done, and are doing it, never shun being seen doing it, even though the multitude should be likely to judge the matter amiss. For if you are not acting rightly, shun the act itself; if rightly, however, why fear misplaced censure?

CLXXIII

It stamps a man of mean capacity to spend much time on the things of the body, as to be long over bodily exercises, long over eating, long over drinking, long over other bodily functions. Rather should these things take the second place, while all your care is directed to the understanding.

CLXXIV

Everything has two handles, one by which it may be borne, the other by which it may not. If your brother sin against you lay not hold of it by the handle of injustice, for by that it may not be borne: but rather by this, that he is your brother, the comrade of your youth; and thus you will lay hold on it so that it may be borne.

CLXXV

Never call yourself a Philosopher nor talk much among the unlearned about Principles, but do that which follows from them. Thus at a banquet, do not discuss how people ought to eat; but eat as you ought. Remember that Socrates thus entirely avoided ostentation. Men would come to him desiring to be recommended to philosophers, and he would conduct them thither himself—so well did he bear being overlooked. Accordingly if any talk concerning principles should arise among the unlearned, be you for the most part silent. For you run great risk of spewing up what you have ill digested. And when a man tells you that you know nothing and you are not nettled at it, then you may be sure that you have begun the work.

CLXXVI

When you have brought yourself to supply the needs of the body at small cost, do not pique yourself on that, nor if you drink only water, keep saying on each occasion, I drink water! And if you ever want to practise endurance and toil, do so unto yourself and not unto others—do not embrace statues!

CLXXVII

When a man prides himself on being able to understand and interpret the writings of Chrysippus, say to yourself:—

If Chrysippus had not written obscurely, this fellow would have had nothing to be proud of. But what is it that I desire? To understand Nature, and to follow her! Accordingly I ask who is the Interpreter. On hearing that it is Chrysippus, I go to him. But it seems I do not understand what he wrote. So I seek one to interpret that. So far there is nothing to pride myself on. But when I have found my interpreter, what remains is to put in practice his instructions. This itself is the only thing to be proud of. But if I admire the interpretation and that alone, what else have I turned out but a mere commentator instead of a lover of wisdom?—except indeed that I happen to be interpreting Chrysippus instead of Homer. So when any one says to me, Prithee, read me Chrysippus, I am more inclined to blush, when I cannot show my deeds to be in harmony and accordance with his sayings.

CLXXVIII

At feasts, remember that you are entertaining two guests, body and soul. What you give to the body, you presently lose; what you give to the soul, you keep for ever.

CLXXIX

At meals, see to it that those who serve be not more in number than those who are served. It is absurd for a crowd of persons to be dancing attendance on half a dozen chairs.

CLXXX

It is best to share with your attendants what is going forward, both in the labour of preparation and in the enjoyment of the feast itself. If such a thing be difficult at the time, recollect that you who are not weary are being served by those that are; you who are eating and drinking by those who do neither; you who are talking by those who are silent; you who are at ease by those who are under constraint. Thus no sudden wrath will betray you into unreasonable conduct, nor will you behave harshly by irritating another.

CLXXXI

When Xanthippe was chiding Socrates for making scanty preparation for entertaining his friends, he answered:—"If they are friends of ours they will not care for that; if they are not, we shall care nothing for them!"

CLXXXII

Asked, Who is the rich man? Epictetus replied, "He who is content."

CLXXXIII

Favorinus tells us how Epictetus would also say that there were two faults far graver and fouler than any others—inability to bear, and inability to forbear, when we neither patiently bear the blows that must be borne, nor abstain from the things and the pleasures we ought to abstain from. "So," he went on, "if a man will only have these two words at heart, and heed them carefully by ruling and watching over himself, he will for the most part fall into no sin, and his life will be tranquil and serene." He meant the words [Greek: Anechou kai apechou]— "Bear and Forbear."

CLXXXIV

On all occasions these thoughts should be at hand:—
    Lead me, O God, and Thou, O Destiny
    Be what it may the goal appointed me,
    Bravely I'll follow; nay, and if I would not,
    I'd prove a coward, yet must follow still!
Again:
    Who to Necessity doth bow aright,
    Is learn'd in wisdom and the things of God.
Once more:—
    Crito, if this be God's will, so let it be. As for me,
    Anytus and Meletus can indeed put me to death, but injure me,
        never!

CLXXXV

We shall then be like Socrates, when we can indite hymns of praise to the Gods in prison.

CLXXXVI

It is hard to combine and unite these two qualities, the

carefulness of one who is affected by circumstances, and the intrepidity of one who heeds them not. But it is not impossible: else were happiness also impossible. We should act as we do in seafaring.

"What can I do?"—Choose the master, the crew, the day, the opportunity. Then comes a sudden storm. What matters it to me? my part has been fully done. The matter is in the hands of another—the Master of the ship. The ship is foundering. What then have I to do? I do the only thing that remains to me—to be drowned without fear, without a cry, without upbraiding God, but knowing that what has been born must likewise perish. For I am not Eternity, but a human being—a part of the whole, as an hour is part of the day. I must come like the hour, and like the hour must pass!

CLXXXVII

And now we are sending you to Rome to spy out the land; but none send a coward as such a spy, that, if he hear but a noise and see a shadow moving anywhere, loses his wits and comes flying to say, The enemy are upon us!

So if you go now, and come and tell us: "Everything at Rome is terrible: Death is terrible, Exile is terrible, Slander is terrible, Want is terrible; fly, comrades! the enemy are upon us!" we shall reply, Get you gone, and prophesy to yourself! we have but erred in sending such a spy as you. Diogenes, who was sent as a spy long before you, brought us back another report than this. He says that Death is no evil; for it need not even bring shame with it. He says that Fame is but the empty noise of madmen. And what report did this spy bring us of Pain, what of Pleasure, what of Want? That to be clothed in sackcloth is better than any purple robe; that sleeping on the bare ground is the softest couch; and in proof of each assertion he points to his own courage, constancy, and freedom; to his own healthy and muscular frame. "There is no enemy near," he cries, "all is perfect peace!"

CLXXXVIII

If a man has this peace—not the peace proclaimed by Cæsar (how indeed should he have it to proclaim?), nay, but the peace proclaimed by God through reason, will not that suffice him when alone, when he beholds and reflects:—Now can no evil happen unto me; for me there is no robber, for me no earthquake; all things are full of peace, full of tranquillity; neither highway nor city nor gathering of men, neither neighbor nor comrade can do me hurt. Another supplies my food, whose care it is; another my raiment; another hath given me perceptions of sense and primary conceptions. And when He supplies my necessities no more, it is that He is sounding the retreat, that He hath opened the door, and is saying to thee, Come!—Wither? To nought that thou needest fear, but to the friendly kindred elements whence thou didst spring. Whatsoever of fire is in thee, unto fire shall return; whatsoever of earth, unto earth; of spirit, unto spirit; of water, unto water. There is no Hades, no fabled rivers of Sighs, of Lamentation, or of Fire: but all things are full of Beings spiritual and divine. With thoughts like these, beholding the Sun, Moon, and Stars, enjoying earth and sea, a man is neither helpless nor alone!

CLXXXIX

What wouldst thou be found doing when overtaken by Death? If I might choose, I would be found doing some deed of true humanity, of wide import, beneficent and noble. But if I may not be found engaged in aught so lofty, let me hope at least for this—what none may hinder, what is surely in my power—that I may be found raising up in myself that which had fallen; learning to deal more wisely with the things of sense; working out my own tranquillity, and thus rendering that which is its due to every relation of life. . . .

If death surprise me thus employed, it is enough if I can

stretch forth my hands to God and say, "The faculties which I received at Thy hands for apprehending this thine Administration, I have not neglected. As far as in me lay, I have done Thee no dishonour. Behold how I have used the senses, the primary conceptions which Thous gavest me. Have I ever laid anything to Thy charge? Have I ever murmured at aught that came to pass, or wished it otherwise? Have I in anything transgressed the relations of life? For that Thou didst beget me, I thank Thee for that Thou hast given: for the time during which I have used the things that were Thine, it suffices me. Take them back and place them wherever Thou wilt! They were all Thine, and Thou gavest them me."—If a man depart thus minded, is it not enough? What life is fairer and more noble, what end happier than his?

(APPENDIX A)

Fragments Attributed to Epictetus

I

A life entangled with Fortune is like a torrent. It is turbulent and muddy; hard to pass and masterful of mood: noisy and of brief continuance.

II

The soul that companies with Virtue is like an ever-flowing source. It is a pure, clear, and wholesome draught; sweet, rich, and generous of its store; that injures not, neither destroys.

III

It is a shame that one who sweetens his drink with the gifts of the bee, should embitter God's gift Reason with vice.

IV

Crows pick out the eyes of the dead, when the dead have no longer need of them; but flatterers mar the soul of the living, and her eyes they blind.

V

Keep neither a blunt knife nor an ill-disciplined looseness of tongue.

VI

Nature hath given men one tongue but two ears, that we may hear from others twice as much as we speak.

VII

Do not give sentence in another tribunal till you have been yourself judged in the tribunal of Justice.

VIII

If is shameful for a Judge to be judged by others.

IX

Give me by all means the shorter and nobler life, instead of one that is longer but of less account!

X

Freedom is the name of virtue: Slavery, of vice. . . . None is a slave whose acts are free.

XI

Of pleasures, those which occur most rarely give the most delight.

XII

Exceed due measure, and the most delightful things become the least delightful.

XIII

The anger of an ape—the threat of a flatterer:—these deserve equal regard.

XIV

Chastise thy passions that they avenge not themselves upon thee.

XV

No man is free who is not master of himself.

XVI

A ship should not ride on a single anchor, nor life on a single hope.

XVII

Fortify thyself with contentment: that is an impregnable stronghold.

XVIII

No man who is a lover of money, of pleasure, of glory, is likewise a lover of Men; but only he that is a lover of whatsoever things are fair and good.

XIX

Think of God more often than thou breathest.

XX

Choose the life that is noblest, for custom can make it sweet to thee.

XXI

Let thy speech of God be renewed day by day, aye, rather than thy meat and drink.

XXII

Even as the Sun doth not wait for prayers and incantations to rise, but shines forth and is welcomed by all: so thou also wait not for clapping of hands and shouts and praise to do thy duty; nay, do good of thine own accord, and thou wilt be loved like the Sun.

XXIII

Let no man think that he is loved by any who loveth none.

XXIV

If thou rememberest that God standeth by to behold and visit all that thou doest; whether in the body or in the soul, thou surely wilt not err in any prayer or deed; and thou shalt have God to dwell with thee.

Note.—Schweighüser's great edition collects 181 fragments attributed to Epictetus, of which but a few are certainly genuine. Some (as xxi., xxiv., above) bear the stamp of Pythagorean origin; others, though changed in form, may well be based upon Epictetean sayings. Most have been preserved in the Anthology of John of Stobi (Stobæus), a Byzantine collector, of whom scarcely anything is known but that he probably wrote towards the end of the fifth century, and made his vast body of extracts from more than five hundred authors for his son's use. The best examination of the authenticity of the Fragments is Quaestiones Epicteteæ, by R. Asmus, 1888. The above selection includes some of doubtful origin but intrinsic interest.—Crossley.

THE HYMN OF CLEANTHES

Chiefest glory of deathless Gods, Almighty for ever,
Sovereign of Nature that rulest by law, what Name shall we give Thee?--
Blessed be Thou! for on Thee should call all things that are mortal.
For that we are Thine offspring; nay, all that in myriad motion
Lives for its day on the earth bears one impress--Thy likeness--upon it.
Wherefore my song is of Thee, and I hymn thy power for ever.

Lo, the vast orb of the Worlds, round the Earth evermore as it rolleth,
Feels Thee its Ruler and Guide, and owns Thy lordship rejoicing.
Aye, for Thy conquering hands have a servant of living fire--
Sharp is the bolt!--where it falls, Nature shrinks at the shock
and doth shudder.
Thus Thou directest the Word universal that pulses through all things,
Mingling its life with Lights that are great and Lights that are lesser,
E'en as beseemeth its birth, High King through ages unending.

Nought is done that is done without Thee in the earth or the waters
Or in the heights of heaven, save the deed of the fool and the sinner.
Thou canst make rough things smooth; at Thy voice, lo, jarring disorder
Moveth to music, and Love is born where hatred abounded.
Thus hast Thou fitted alike things good and things evil together,
That over all might reign one Reason, supreme and eternal;
Though thereunto the hearts of the wicked be hardened and heedless--
Woe unto them!--for while ever their hands are grasping at good things,
Blind are their eyes, yea, stopped are their ears to God's Law universal,

Calling through wise disobedience to live the life that is noble.
This they mark not, but heedless of right, turn each to his own way,
Here, a heart fired with ambition, in strife and straining unhallowed;
There, thrusting honour aside, fast set upon getting and gaining;
Others again given over to lusts and dissolute softness,
Working never God's Law, but that which warreth upon it.

Nay, but, O Giver of all things good, whose home is the dark cloud,
Thou that wieldesy Heaven's bolt, save men from their ignorance grievous;
Scatter its night from their souls, and grant them to come to that Wisdom
Wherewithal, sistered with Justice, Thou rulest and governest all things;
That we, honoured by Thee, may requite Thee with worship and honour,
Evermore praising thy works, as is meet for men that shall perish;
Seeing that none, be he mortal or God, hath privilege nobler
Than without stint, without stay, to extol Thy Law universal.

www.ingramcontent.com/pod-product-compliance
Lightning Source LLC
Chambersburg PA
CBHW031812220426
43662CB00007B/607